Collecting Pe[bbles]
and F[ossils]

Wherever you live you can be sure that not very far away you'll be able to discover and collect dozens of interesting pebbles, rocks and fossils. This book tells you where to look for them, how to identify and classify your finds, and then deals with storing and displaying the fossils and polishing the pebbles and rocks you've found. There are also suggestions on what to do with the more attractive rocks, from making simple jewellery to mosaics. Finally, there's a chapter on museums in which you can see all sorts of fascinating rocks and fossils and one that lists lots of useful addresses to help you in your new hobby. If this book doesn't make you a 'rock hound', then nothing will!

George Kay has written a large number of books for both children and adults, including *The Beaver Book of Games* and *Everybody's Birthday Book*.

Collecting
PEBBLES,
ROCKS & FOSSILS

George Kay

Illustrated by Valerie Jones

Beaver Books

First published in 1980 by
The Hamlyn Publishing Group Limited
London · New York · Sydney · Toronto
Astronaut House, Feltham, Middlesex, England

© Copyright Text George Kay 1980
© Copyright Illustrations
The Hamlyn Publishing Group Limited 1980
ISBN 0 600 32181 9

Set, printed and bound in Great Britain by
Cox & Wyman Ltd, Reading
Set in Monotype Imprint

Contents

1 The Stories in Stones

We all like collecting things – stamps, coins, autographs, special kinds of toys, books, photos, records, or motor car names and numbers.

Some collecting hobbies are expensive. Some get boring as you get older. But collecting pebbles means that almost everywhere you go there is a possible new addition to your display, and you will not get tired of your hobby because it combines plenty of outdoor activity as well as interesting hours at home, preparing and arranging your trophies. It's almost certain that, once you start as a pebble hunter, you will continue long after you have grown up, and may even become an expert on the secrets locked up in stones.

In the United States, where any fine day sees thousands of people, young and old, at the coasts, lakes, deserts and rivers enjoying another search, pebble collectors are called 'rock hounds'. There are clubs, magazines, and exhibitions to help along the interest and create friendships among people who are fascinated by all those masses of little pebbles which less lively folk think of as – just stones.

Pebbles are much more than small bits of stone or rock, smooth and rounded. When you know more about the Earth on which we live, you will see that each has its own long history to reveal.

You may start collecting pebbles because of their different colours and shapes, because some have beautiful and curious patterns, or because they are souvenirs of a happy time at the seaside or in the country.

Those are good reasons to start a collection, but they will not make your interest in them grow as it would if you selected pebbles because you know there are rare ones, quite valuable ones, and many more that are quite different in origin and substance from one another.

There are very few places where pebbles do not exist. Sandy beaches are made up of ground-down pebbles, so somewhere in the area or just below the surface of the sand you will find them. They lie concealed in the muddy banks of streams and mixed with the soil of farmlands and gardens. Even in towns and cities there are plenty of pebbles, because they are used in such enormous quantities to construct buildings and roads.

We talk about stones and pieces of rock as well as pebbles, so when deciding to collect pebbles we need to decide just what a pebble is. Most collectors would say that any stone which is smooth and round, oval or flat, as small as a pea or as large as a tennis ball can be called a pebble. Those are good rules as a basis for your collection, but there will be times when you want to keep a small piece which is quite jagged as the result of a recent breakage, or will be broken up by yourself to display its patterned interior. If your find can be held easily in your clasped hand you will be right to include it in your collection no matter what its shape, though more usually you will prefer a pebble which is no larger than a walnut and maybe as small as a pea.

Doubtless the majority of your pebbles will have a smooth surface without any corners. How did they get like that?

Mainly, but not always, they have been shaped by the action of water and weather. Every pebble began its existence in a huge mass of rock.

Some started their slow shaping anything from 20 thousand million to 600 thousand million years ago. During that long period four ice ages occurred, covering the British Isles almost as far south as London and Bristol and extending all the way to the North Pole. The ice sheets were a mile thick in places, and the enormous weight created glaciers which rumbled slowly towards the warmer areas where they began to melt.

These glaciers were not just masses of ice, but contained trees, dead animals, mud, and rocks – anything which they passed over. The roughened ice scraped the sides of mountains, ripping away more lumps of rock and grinding the pieces one against another until they were broken up, sometimes into powder which combined with soil to become clay, but just as often into smaller and smaller pieces of stone.

When the ice receded after the Earth warmed up again, the land and the seabed were strewn with countless pebbles, large stones and massive boulders.

That was just the first stage in the pebble's development. The bits of rock left below the surface of the sea were gradually worn away by water action. The friction of the tides rubbed one piece against another until they became small enough to be carried by currents towards the shore where the waves threw them up on the beaches, only to wash them out to sea again as the tide receded.

The mass of debris left on the land – on hills, mountains and in valleys – was attacked by weather and water. The heat of the sun caused some parts of a boulder to expand faster than the rest of it, creating cracks. Winter's frost and ice widened these cracks until the boulder split into pieces.

Rain, wind and the contours of the ground caused the smaller pieces to be carried to a stream or river, where the slow process of shaping and moving continued, eventually carrying the young and newly formed pebbles to the sea or depositing them in deep parts of the rivers and along their banks.

For some pebbles, banked up in great layers of gravel or mud, the long period of changing shape was over. They remained buried under soil until a change in the course of a river or an exceptionally high tide on the coast exposed them, or man dug down to extract them for use in building and road-making.

Not all pebbles are as old as these. Those in mountain streams or on the beaches may have been parts of rock only a few centuries ago. Millions of the pebbles of the future are beginning their formation this year. Most are being produced where the sea batters against the cliffs in stormy weather. The waves hurl themselves at the base of the cliff, bits of stone aiding the pressure of water in the attack, until cracks in the cliff appear and finally lumps fall off.

This undercutting weakens the higher levels of the cliff and they too crash down and break into pieces. Day after day lumps of rock, large and small, are rubbed against one another until they are reduced in size and all the jagged edges are smoothed away.

Yet these nicely rounded and pretty pebbles you may pick up on the beach will not remain in those shapes for ever. In a way you are collecting something only part of the way through its life.

In time, perhaps thousands or millions of years ahead, according to its hardness and the conditions existing where it lies, a pebble will be ground smaller and smaller until it becomes sand, and then perhaps begin yet another cycle of existence, buried and compressed until it again becomes a mass of rock.

As you begin collecting pebbles, and study some of them by breaking them open against one another or with a hammer, seeing if you can scratch the surface with the point of a knife, you will realise that differences are not only those of colour and shape, but of hardness. Pebbles which break easily or have a surface covered in scratch marks are obviously newer than those which are very difficult to break and are quite heavy.

Now you are beginning to learn that there is a lot more in the story of pebbles than you imagined. Later in this book we will explore the ways in which so many different kinds of pebbles were created. Knowing all this won't really affect your new hobby as regards making a start. You can pick up pebbles that you like the look of, and make them reveal their story later. The great thing is to obtain a varied selection as soon as you can. That way you will have become a collector.

Many of the pebbles you pick up at first will be of the same stone, but don't worry. Later, you can go over your finds and choose the best of any one kind. But don't throw out a pebble just because it looks much like another. Perhaps you have found two almost identical pebbles in very different places, and this information can be interesting in proving how one area is the same geologically as another quite a distance away, or it will indicate how pebbles move long distances from the places where they originated.

Every find you make can produce its own history. Make notes as soon as you can after finding a pebble. Write down the date, the location, whether it was just one of hundreds of the same kind or a stranger among others, and any other incident which will help you to remember that occasion, perhaps years afterwards.

If you want a good record of your searches buy a map, or better still, if you intend to search a long way from home when you visit other places on holiday, buy two maps – one of your home area and one of the British Isles.

The best maps are those published by the Ordnance Survey. You can buy them at any good bookseller, and they will be able to order area maps if you want them. Or you can write to the Ordnance Survey, Romsey Road, Maybush, Southampton, and ask for a list of all the maps available.

Pin your maps on the wall of your bedroom or playroom if you can. That is much better than keeping them folded up. Mark the spots where you have found the pebbles you intend to keep with a blob of coloured ink or crayon, and beside the blob write a number. Your very first find will thus be marked 1, the second 2, and so on.

Next you need a stiff-covered student's exercise book or, if you prefer, one with loose leaves. It should have at least 100 pages so that you can make one entry on each page.

At the top of the page write down the number you have put on your map. Then below it write the date; place; details of the type of ground (shingle or sandy seashore, river bank, field, gravel pit, pile of rubble and so on – any detail which will help to revive your memory of the find); the geology of the area if you know it (limestone, clay, chalk, and so on); the kind of stone (you may not be sure so you may add a question mark or some such comment as 'probably granite'); and finally any remarks you like on how the pebble may have originated (don't forget that other people will be interested in your collection and will not know as much about pebbles as you do, so that when they look at your pebbles, or

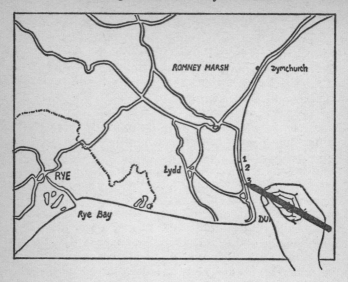

maps, and open the record book they will be interested to learn about the pebbles' history).

As so many pebbles are similar in appearance and you will have many that are of the same stone, you will need to mark each pebble with the same number as that on the map and in your record book.

Sticky paper rarely sticks for ever and soon gets grimy, and the surface of some pebbles will not take a label of this kind. It is much better to mark the pebble with the number in ink or chinagraph pencil. You can buy a cheap ballpoint pen with ink that will write on any surface but is washable should you ever wish to change the number. Chinagraph pencils, which will even write on glass, are also good but it is difficult to remove the marking without leaving a smear. To get rid of all traces, the pebble would have to be rubbed with a piece of cotton wool dipped in turpentine substitute, which is also called white spirit.

Most pebbles need to be soaked in warm water for a few hours and then left to dry. This applies particularly to those

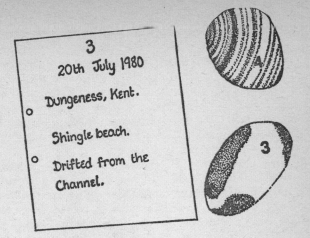

3

20th July 1980

° Dungeness, Kent.

Shingle beach.

° Drifted from the Channel.

How to record and mark your pebble finds

you take from the seashore. There will be salt deposits, and unless you wash away the salt there will be a white film on the surface after the pebble has been kept dry for some time.

When deciding which pebbles you will keep remember that you will almost always want to have two of every kind. If you find one with a fossil in it, the total will be three. You will learn how to recognise fossils on pages 35–48.

The reason for collecting at least two of a kind is to examine both the outside and the inside of the pebble. Many pebbles get a thin covering on the surface due to the presence of sand, mud, chemicals and the action of water. Loose dirt should be removed by washing in warm water containing some washing-up liquid, using an old toothbrush to scrub the surface gently. But don't do too much washing or you may change the pebble's natural appearance.

This covering, even when cleaned up, will not reveal the appearance of the stone before it was shaped and smoothed. To know what its original appearance was like you need to show the surface inside. Some pebbles will not split or crack easily because the material is so hard, though in this case the surface will not have changed as it will have resisted the friction caused by other pebbles and by water.

Most pebbles, however, will break quite easily if placed on a hard surface, such as a flat stone or strong concrete, and given a smart tap with a hammer. You need to learn the knack of hitting the pebble with just enough force to break it, but not so heavily that it breaks into several tiny pieces. At first, therefore, you should bring a few extra specimens of the same kind so that you can experiment.

The freshly exposed inner surface of a broken pebble will usually be much more colourful than the smooth outer surface and will tell you much more about the rock from which it was formed. Some pebbles, such as coarse sandstone (brown outside and pink inside) or serpentine, may look uninteresting where the surface has been changed by weathering, but will reveal beautiful colours when cracked open.

Of course, you never break a pebble with a fossil clearly seen on the surface. But it is well worth while collecting likely specimens of such easily broken stone as shale, sandstone, slate, and limestone, and breaking them open just to see whether you will have the good fortune to expose a fossil hidden inside.

Most collectors are quite content to list their pebbles in the order they find them. But you may prefer to be really scientific and start on a career as an amateur mineralogist, keeping your pebbles listed separately according to the main class of rock from which they came.

In this case the numbers on the maps should be in three different colours, say black, red and green, and you should use three separate books for the details. You will understand why you need three books after we have explored the main groups of rock from which the earth's surface is formed.

You will need to become quite expert to be certain that you can identify the group to which a pebble belongs. Before you make a definite decision it would be wise to ask the advice of someone at a museum, or to compare your pebble with that in a display where pieces of stone and pebbles are labelled.

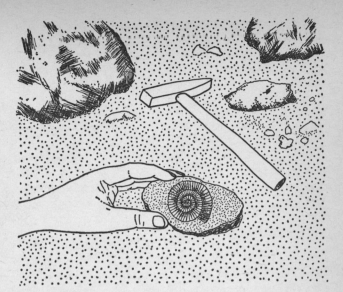

Sometimes breaking open a piece of rock will expose a
fossil like this ammonite

Still further variations of the map-and-book record of
your hobby is to keep entirely separate lists of fossils and
those extra-special finds: semi-precious gemstones. You
could mark your map with numbers in blue for fossils, and
in yellow for semi-precious gemstones.

Later on in this book you will see some ideas for displaying
your collection. As a beginning use a box with a lid – a
chocolate or shoe box, or one of those shallow plastic con-
tainers used for storing biscuits and cakes.

Put a layer of cotton wool about three centimetres thick on
the bottom, so that you can make little indentations in it for
your pebbles, thus ensuring that they do not rub together
when the box is moved. Another good idea is to use the
cardboard or plastic trays in which eggs are sold. You can

easily cut them up to fit your box, or add sections of a tray to fill the space. Then you need only a thin layer of cotton wool to cover the tray, and the spaces for eggs are just about the right size for pebbles.

If you intend to arrange your collection according to the groups of rock then you will need a separate box for each. Before we talk about those groups of rocks which were the pebbles' 'parents' here are some do's and don'ts about your first expedition as a pebble collector.

2 Do's and Don'ts

Like most activities, pebble collecting involves a few rules and regulations. 'Do this' and 'don't do that' may sound annoying when talking about a hobby which is intended to give you plenty of fun, but these simple rules are worth heeding so that you do enjoy yourselves in safety.

It is more fun to go pebble hunting with a friend or two, but if you go off by yourself always let someone know the places you intend to explore and roughly how long you expect to be away. With the hope that there will be another good find a little way ahead it is very easy to wander farther than you intended and to be away from home longer than you said.

Very often your searches will be at the seaside because beaches are the best source of every kind of pebble. Unless you live on the coast or have visited a resort many times previously you will be exploring unknown and potentially dangerous territory.

Get to know the times of high and low tides. Start your search just after high tide. A newly washed beach exposes previously hidden pebbles, and you will know that you have several hours in which to search before the tide rises again.

Be extra careful when moving along a coast bordered by high cliffs and little bays. If you pass a headland at low tide you may find it impossible to return that way a long time before high tide.

Cliffs undercut by the sea during winter storms may have exciting pebbles and fossils in the debris below them, lying as rubble on the beach. You may even see an attractive find in the surface of the cliffs face right before your eyes or a metre or so higher up.

It is tempting to try to reach it and loosen it. Don't do so without a grown-up to advise and help. The fact that the pebble or fossil has been recently exposed proves that the material of the cliff is insecure. You can easily bring tons of rock crashing down if you dislodge the lower rocks. Sadly, people are hurt every year by causing cliff falls like this when they hammer at the cliff face or, worse, try to climb it.

In most areas where cliffs are liable to fall there are danger notices. Don't ignore them, particularly after heavy rain or in winter, when there has been frost and snow. Rainwater percolating down from the top of the cliffs can force its way out through the cliff face, bringing down masses of rock. Frost may split off large lumps which fall when there is a thaw.

The beach between high and low tide marks belongs to the Queen and is free to everybody. The land behind it may be private. You must keep to public footpaths and roads unless you get permission to cross it.

The same rule about private property applies to quarries, gravel pits and areas including working or disused mines. When parts of quarries and gravel pits are filled with water remember that the water is usually very deep and the sides of lakes and ponds may be almost vertical. There is no chance of paddling along the edge as in some natural lakes and rivers.

Mine tips are often steep. Climbing up them in dry weather can cause a mass of debris to move. When the material is wet it can be even more dangerous, and your feet may start an avalanche of sticky, cloying sludge. That is why quarries, gravel pits, and mine tips may be fenced off and trespassers are liable to prosecution. You will almost always need to get permission to go searching in these areas and then only if an adult accompanies you.

As a matter of fact, it is better to go pebble hunting in gravel pits and quarries when men are working in them. There will be an office at the gate where the manager or foreman can tell you whether you may enter. He will know the safe places, and there will be workmen to keep an eye out for you.

In some places there are mines which have long since been abandoned. Fences have been broken and entrances to shafts are overgrown with bushes and trees. Although the debris from such old mines, such as those in the Forest of Dean and in Cornwall, may yield stones which are rarely found elsewhere, they should never be visited except in the company of an adult who knows the area well. This warning also applies to the cave districts of Derbyshire and Yorkshire, where even experienced potholers sometimes suffer accidents when they fall into crevices almost hidden by undergrowth and tall grass.

When you go pebble searching inland, in fields and along streams, remember that someone owns the property even if there is a public footpath. Do not damage hedges and fences. Shut all field gates after you have passed through. Keep off growing crops and avoid disturbing cattle and sheep.

After all these warnings, which should not put you off pebble hunting in unfamiliar places but will ensure that you have a happy and successful time, here are some hints about the kit you need.

A small haversack will leave your hands free. Wear shoes with good, non-slip soles. You will probably go barefoot on some parts of the seashore but it will hurt to walk on shingle beaches and rocks can be slippery. Take a showerproof anorak or a plastic macintosh unless the morning sky makes it absolutely certain that the day is going to be a beautifully sunny one.

If you are going to be out for two or three hours you will get hungry and thirsty. Sweets make you thirstier still, so it is better to have some fruit to go with a bread roll, some cake, or a few sandwiches with lettuce included with the other filling. Water and tea are more thirst-quenching than sweet, fizzy drinks.

Broken pebbles, shells and some rocks can have jagged edges. A minor cut on your probing fingers won't trouble you if you have a few strips of Elastoplast in your kit.

Keep your actual collecting items to a minimum to save weight and avoid those lumpy bits that rub against your back

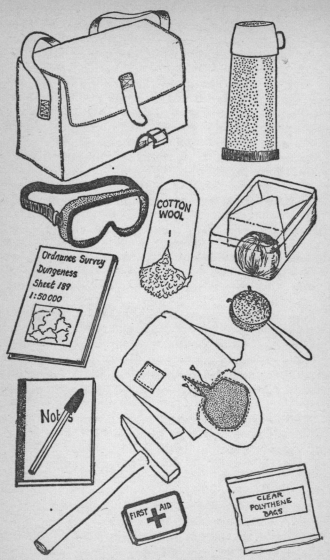

Some of the things to take with you on a pebble and fossil hunting expedition

through the haversack. A small hammer is useful. There are special geological hammers, but any small hammer with a flat head and a point at the other end of the head will be all that you need to prise specimens from a rock or break a pebble.

A dozen or so small plastic bags will be needed for your finds. You can buy them in stationers and supermarkets but there is really no need to spend money on them. Your mother will get these bags in all sorts of sizes with her purchases of food.

Clean up your pebble as much as you can, put it in its own bag and write on the bag with a felt-tip pen with ink that adheres to plastic. A number is all that you need write down. Then stop for a minute or two and jot down date, place, probable name of pebble, and any other details you think will be worth recording in a notebook.

There are one or two extras you may think are worth taking along. If you are exploring on a sandy or muddy shore you may want to sift through it for very small but rare stones, such as semi-precious gemstones or fossils. A coffee strainer or flour sifter is quite bulky but light in weight. If you come across fossils which can be very fragile some cotton wool will be useful to protect them inside the bag.

Finally, don't forget to take a map of the district if you intend to be out for some time. It will show you attractive places where pebbles are likely to be found, and will also indicate footpaths and roads so you do not find your intended route blocked by rivers, fenced areas, and other obstacles.

3 The Secrets of the Rocks

The day you begin collecting pebbles you will be impressed, perhaps for the first time, by how many different kinds there are. What once were almost ignored as 'just little stones' seem to be almost as varied as the living creatures and plants you see around the shingle or rocky landscape.

So that you can identify the pebbles you pick up, and recognise the appearance of areas where particular kinds will be found, you will need to know something about geology, which is the word for the study of the crust of the earth – the land we live on.

You probably have an atlas, or can look at one in school, which includes a geological map with the different kinds of material forming the land shown in contrasting colours. There will also be maps of this kind in your local library which will give the geological information in more detail just for a small area. Better still are the regional handbooks on sale at the Geological Museum, Exhibition Road, South Kensington, London SW7 2DE. They can also be obtained from Her Majesty's Stationery Office (HMSO) bookshops in large towns, and any bookseller can order them for you. These handbooks include maps, pictures, and many details which will help you to hunt for and identify pebbles successfully.

Before you try to understand maps and books of this kind it will help to know why there are so many different kinds of landscape, even in a small country like the British Isles.

The whole surface of the earth is covered in rock much as a skin covers an orange – a skin about forty kilometres thick. Except where there are mountains, cliffs and high hills

The geology of Britain

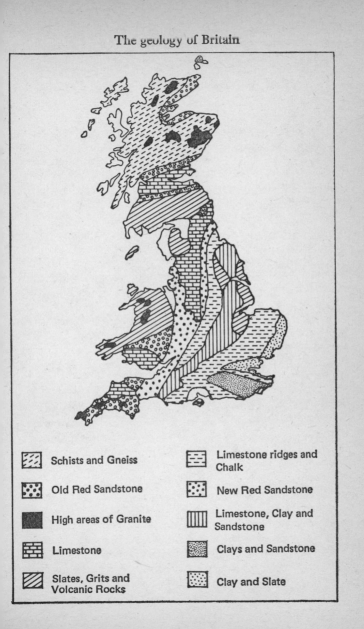

Schists and Gneiss		Limestone ridges and Chalk
Old Red Sandstone		New Red Sandstone
High areas of Granite		Limestone, Clay and Sandstone
Limestone		Clays and Sandstone
Slates, Grits and Volcanic Rocks		Clay and Slate

most of the rock is hidden under soil and vegetation, or covered by the sea which surrounds the land. The material in which vegetation can grow is merely rock broken into small grains, changed by weathering, the action of bacteria and chemicals, moved by rivers, and cultivated by man.

About half of the world's skin is composed of granite, which is an igneous rock.

The name 'igneous' means that these rocks were formed in the world's interior furnace, and so high is the temperature that as they emerged from the interior of the earth they were liquid. You may have seen films of lava moving down the sides of a volcano during an eruption. Hardened lava is an example of an igneous rock.

The most common kind of granite is that which you can see almost everywhere in use as a building material. It is usually pale grey in colour. If you look more closely you will see that it is speckled with white, black and pale red. The speckles are crystals of minerals – quartz, giving the grey colour; feldspar, white or pale red; and mica, black – giving granite its sparkle when light shines on it.

Granite was formed millions of years ago deep below the earth's surface, where the heat melted everything. Thrust upwards in volcanoes and earthquakes, the thick, lumpy liquid cooled quite slowly, turning into masses of crystals stuck together.

You can understand just how fine debris, mixed with sea water and then subjected to tremendous heat from the earth's fiery interior, turned into the coarse grains of the granite we see today if you watch someone boiling sugar. Originally the sugar has fine grains. Mixed in cold water, it dissolves. Heated until almost all the water has evaporated the sugar turns into large crystals if it is allowed to cool slowly.

That is what happened when granite was formed. It may have taken many years to cool and solidify. Granite is very hard, but weather, water and chemicals can soften or destroy some of the minerals which granite contains. Then it breaks up, first into smaller rocks, then into stones and pebbles, and eventually into grains of sand when, if it is again subjected to pressure, it will become hardened rock once more.

You are unlikely to find a pebble of granite which is nicely rounded and smooth because of the rock's hardness and the probability that a small piece will break up because of changes in the minerals it contains. But small pieces can be collected which have great variety because of the different minerals in them.

There are some other rocks which, like granite, were formed deep inside the earth and forced towards the surface. Some are difficult to identify unless you compare them with specimens in a museum.

Diorite is not so rough-looking as granite and is rather darker in colour. In Scotland it is called 'greenstone' because of its patchy green colour.

Gabbro also has a green tinge, but is paler than diorite. The background colour is dark grey.

Basalt is formed from such tiny crystals that they are invisible unless you examine it under a microscope. The reason that basalt does not have the roughness of granite is that after the liquid reached the surface cold air and water hardened it before large crystals could form. A basalt pebble appears to be an uninteresting black stone, but it can be polished and given an attractive sheen.

The next group of rocks to consider are called metamorphic, a word which means that they have changed their form since they were first created. A simpler description of them is 'transformed' rocks.

When the young world was still restless, with enormous quantities of molten material coming to the surface, the rocks already on or near the surface were heated again and again, hurled upwards to form mountains, brought crashing down and ground into debris, buried, and once more compressed into rocks.

Slate is one kind of transformed rock. It was once clay which was changed under enormous pressure. Slate has the property of breaking into thin flat sheets, so the pebbles you find will be flat and quite easily broken.

White marble is rarely found in Britain, and any small pieces you may pick up were probably thrown out by sculptors or stone-masons. In Derbyshire there is some red or brown marble, and on the island of Tiree off the west coast of Scotland it is pink with green streaks.

Serpentine, like marble, is transformed limestone. It has a beautiful green colour, sometimes with traces of red in it. It got the name serpentine because its surface, before being smoothed in sea water, feels rather like the skin of a snake if you stroke it with your fingers. As you have probably never stroked a snake, the next best description is that the slightly rough surface seems to be waxy.

Gneiss, a German word for 'sparkling' or 'shining' (pronounced 'nice'), has many of the minerals found in granite, but they occur in bands to produce alternate shades of light and dark, green and yellow.

Schist also has its minerals grouped together, and the layers are composed of flakes you can easily break away. The pebble is usually a dull green, sometimes with a silvery sparkle from the mica in it. When you break a schist pebble and look at the irregular and crumpled flakes inside you will have a glimpse of the enormous pressures which formed it.

Quartzite pebbles originated when sand beds or sandstone were subjected to heat so intense that the grains melted and crystallised. The pebbles are smooth, hard, and brown or brown-grey, often with a band of near-white or near-black. When broken, quartzite shatters into small pieces of all shapes and sizes.

Metamorphic or transformed rocks, as we have seen, are largely composed of crystals. Some of the trapped minerals from which the crystals were formed may be those which form gems. Red garnets are the most widely scattered and common in Britain. If you find any semi-precious stone it will have originated in metamorphic rocks.

When we come to talk about fossils you will guess that we are not likely to find any in metamorphic rocks. Some of these rocks were formed before animal or plant life existed on earth. And when the change from one kind of material to another occurred any trapped objects were ground to dust, burned, and obliterated by pressure. Now and then some did manage to leave a few traces. They were changed into graphite and appear as a black smear inside the stone, or even an outline of their shape, but so twisted and distorted that only experts can identify them.

The third group is that of sedimentary rocks. The name indicates that they were formed from sand, stones and other debris sinking down in the sea to lie in an ever-increasing mass of sediment on the seabed, piled up by wind and river currents, or drying out at the edge of the sea and lakes.

Over long periods of time layer after layer of sediment was added. Either by earthquake, the depth of water or the sheer weight of the mass of debris, the material was compressed, with chemical action sticking all the grains of material together to become rock. Eventually it rose above the sea, folding and twisting so that the layers, seen on the face of many cliffs, may follow wavy lines, be broken, or appear almost vertical.

Chalk is the most easily recognised sedimentary rock in England. It consists of grains of minerals and the broken shells of tiny sea creatures. Freshly broken, a piece of chalk is a brilliant white, but in some places, notably near Hunstanton in Norfolk, there are layers of red chalk among the white ones. Buried in the chalk are lumps of flint, black, brown or grey and very hard. Although flint is so different from the chalk in which it is found, it was also formed from the bodies of sea creatures.

Limestone, with materials closely allied to those in chalk, is hard enough to be used for buildings. Its rough-surfaced pebbles can be of many colours – white, cream, grey, brown, and almost black. These two sedimentary rocks are symbols of our land – the chalky white walls of England facing the Straits of Dover and the limestones of the Pennines, called England's backbone. In some varieties of limestone the shells and hard parts of the sea creatures which formed the rock can be seen quite clearly. A shelly or coral limestone pebble is a welcome find among all the flat oval pebbles which have quite a firm surface.

Sandstone is an easily remembered name because it is just like sand which has been pressed together and hardened. Most of it is soft enough to be cut or even scratched with your nail, though pebbles which have been rounded by the sea will be harder. The colours range from grey to yellow and red.

Clay was also part of that sediment from which sedimentary rocks were formed and is really a soft rock. In some places the pressure was great enough to harden clay. It is called 'mudstone', and, though a small piece is dull in colour and not very attractive, it can be added to your collection as an unusual example of a sedimentary rock.

Shale is the last important sedimentary rock. It is a form of clay pressed into very thin layers. The most attractive kind of shale which you may find as a perfectly flat, thin pebble, is blue in colour.

To find specimen pebbles of all these rocks it is useful to know the areas where a particular kind of rock is likely to make up the landscape and to learn how it got there.

The shape of Britain and Ireland as we see it in an atlas or from a satellite photograph is very different from that which it had in the past. Placid and secure as our land may seem now, long, long ago its surface was thrust skywards, twisted, folded, and brought crashing down. It has been high above the sea and deep below it. For immense periods of time most of it was buried deep under ice and snow, and for as long it was largely a swampy forest.

The earliest land eventually to take shape as the British Isles emerged from the sea about 3000 million years ago. A mountain range was forced upwards in what is now the northwest corner of Scotland. The remains of those mountains are in the Hebrides, where the pebbles you can collect are the oldest you will ever find in the British Isles. It has taken 3000 million years for a mountain to be created, great boulders splitting off it to be broken into smaller and smaller pieces, which have been smoothed and rounded by other stones, sand, ice and water, and eventually turned into the pebble in your hand.

Hundreds of millions of years after those first mountains appeared a great mass of rock rose up to form the Scottish Highlands. In many places eruptions sent rivers of molten material through cracks in the rising land, and these became the granite of the Cairngorms. The peaks were much higher than they are today. The boulders and debris torn away by the weather and more earthquakes spread the material across the land to the south and into the seas to the east and west.

All this time the land south of the Highlands and far into England slowly sank, allowing the sea to spread over it. The silt and sand on the sea bed became slowly piled up until the mass was more than a mile thick, being steadily compressed into the sedimentary rocks of shale, limestone and sandstone.

Here and there lava poured skywards, and slowly, for more than 200 million years, the material below the water rose higher and higher until there was another great mountain range, stretching from what are now the lowlands of Scotland across England and most of Wales to Devon and Somerset.

The peaks of this mountain range towered almost as high as the Andes and Himalayas of today. You can see one survivor of these prehistoric mountains in Wales – Snowdon, which is 1080 metres high. Yet the top of Snowdon was once at the bottom of a gap between high peaks. The peaks were torn away but Snowdon's rock was hard enough to survive even though it was later buried under the sea.

This huge mountain range in time almost disappeared because it consisted mainly of the compressed sediment which had been buried below the sea. Torrential rain, hurricane winds, baking heat and terrible cold transformed entire mountains into a reddish brown dust which spread far and wide, turning the land into a desert dotted with muddy lakes and winding rivers.

Here and there the bases of the mountains were not entirely worn away, and you can see them in the Lake District and in the hills and mountains of Wales. The dust, where it was mixed with water, was compressed once again, turning into the red sandstone of the hills of southern Scotland, the Brecon Beacons and the bleak uplands of Exmoor.

The weight of dust and debris from the dead and dying mountains was one reason why once more the land sank down and allowed the sea to flood over it. Billions of tiny marine creatures, combined with minerals in the water, formed masses of limestone over the sandstone. This in its turn was

Snowdon

slowly covered by silt carried down by rivers and rain.

Subterranean forces changed the sea level by pushing the seabed upwards. The climate became warm. The pools, lakes and swamps swarmed with life. Great forests spread, the trees growing quickly, dying, and being replaced by still more trees. The mass of rotting wood was covered by vegetation and mud, slowly sinking down and down until it was deep enough to be compressed by the limestone and shale far below the surface. The material was turned into coal over such an immense area that it is often said that Britain stands on a foundation of coal.

All this time upheavals were also taking place in what is now south, south-east and eastern England. The uplands which stretch from the Yorkshire moors across the Midlands and Cotswolds to the Dorset coast were formed by the invading sea which covered most of the land, leaving masses of limestone when it retreated. That began about 180 million years ago, and the thicker deposits of limestone were only partly covered when once more the land sank below the waves.

When it again rose much of it was covered with a thick deposit of chalk. It is near the surface in the Lincolnshire wolds, part of Yorkshire, Norfolk, the Chiltern Hills, the North and South Downs of Kent, and along much of the coastal area as far as the Isle of Wight and Dorset.

Such hard materials like chalk and limestone could not produce the fertile land we know today. That is largely the result of the fact that, after about 60 million years, most of south-east England yet again sank below the sea, this time remaining a drowned land for more than 50 million years and gathering a thick covering of clay and sand.

More upheavals of the earth then occurred. They were more violent in Europe where they raised the Alps high above the sea. In southern England they created hills and valleys still covered by clay and sand. The hills were far higher than any today and the valleys formed when the earth folded in on itself were steep-sided and deep.

The last great changes began about a million years ago, the period of the great ice ages. Four times the ice came and went, advancing from the North Pole and forming ice fields a mile and more deep, with glaciers sliding southwards, pushing everything before them like enormous bulldozers. Great rocks and boulders were carried from Norway and the Scottish Highlands to England. The moving ice cut into the sides of mountains, grinding the shattered pieces into stones and pebbles, leaving ridges in the mountains and deep valleys in its wake.

Ahead of the end of the glaciers came masses of clay, gravel and sand. The intense cold eased in the south of Britain, and the ice began to melt when it reached the area south of a line from the present Bristol Channel to the mouth of the Thames. Beyond, water melting from the ice, thick with the clay and stones and debris, slowly flowed to the sea, leaving a deposit sometimes 30 metres thick. The last time this happened was about 10,000 years ago.

This long adventure story of the birth of the British Isles helps us to know the areas in which we are most likely to find pebbles of a particular kind, and to identify those we pick up as pieces of igneous, metamorphic, or sedimentary rocks.

The map on page 33 will help you to know what you can expect to find in the area you intend to explore, with a little help from the following descriptive tour of Britain.

Most of the north of Scotland is a land of granite, with patches of other igneous rocks where molten lava burst to the surface and solidified. Those igneous rocks also occur in quite small areas north of Edinburgh, near Berwick-on-Tweed, in the Lake District, in the mountains of Snowdonia, on Dartmoor, and a large area of Northern Ireland.

Southern Scotland and northern England as far as the northerly edge of the Midlands, most of Wales, and Devon and Cornwall stand on sandstone, limestone, shale and slate.

The centre of England, and a wide band stretching from the Yorkshire moors south-westwards to Somerset, is a mixture of limestone, sandstone and clay.

East of that area, chalk, sandstone, sand, and clay form eastern and south-eastern England, starting in Lincolnshire, taking in East Anglia, the London area, Kent, and all the land bordering on the English Channel as far as Weymouth.

There is no need to feel frustrated about the chance of finding new pebbles if you cannot go collecting in an area with a greatly different rock formation from the one in which you live or take your holidays and have picked up all the typical pebbles of those places. Over all that time we have been learning about, rocks, stones and pebbles have constantly moved over huge distances. Nowadays man has speeded up this movement, transporting granite, slate, and sandstone for buildings, mining the earth and carrying the debris to build embankments, digging out clay to make bricks and china, moving millions of tons of gravel for roads, tearing away deposits of chalk to make cement.

You can even come across pebbles which were formed in other lands far across the oceans of the world. When Britain exported coal to ports in every continent, ships came loaded with ballast which nearly always consisted of small stones and gravel, easily obtained at foreign ports and unloaded

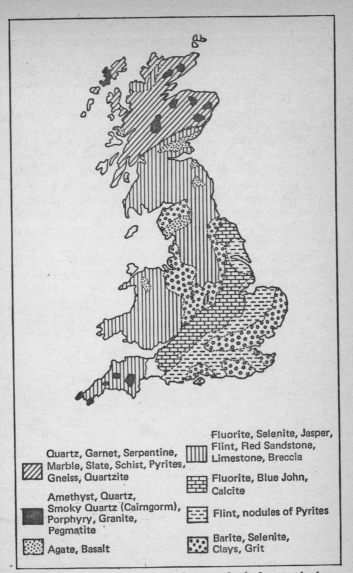

Quartz, Garnet, Serpentine, Marble, Slate, Schist, Pyrites, Gneiss, Quartzite

Amethyst, Quartz, Smoky Quartz (Cairngorm), Porphyry, Granite, Pegmatite

Agate, Basalt

Fluorite, Selenite, Jasper, Flint, Red Sandstone, Limestone, Breccia

Fluorite, Blue John, Calcite

Flint, nodules of Pyrites

Barite, Selenite, Clays, Grit

This map will show you where to look for particular rocks, pebbles and minerals without any problem before the ships took on a fresh cargo of coal. This ballast was dumped in the sea near the coal ports in Scotland, Tyneside and South Wales.

Carmarthen Bay, from Saundersfoot to the Pendine Sands, is a particularly good place to find these 'foreign' pebbles. So many tons of ballast were dumped near Saundersfoot that the stones formed a new beach. The sea has spread the smaller pebbles for miles along the coast.

Don't expect to find many strange-looking pebbles. The rocks of the whole world are much the same wherever you go – mainly granite, limestone and sandstone. But within those groups are nearly 2000 different minerals, many of them not found in Britain. You may therefore pick up a pebble with a pattern, colour, or texture you have never seen before owing to the presence of minerals and the way in which they affected the rock.

If you do, you will have yet another addition to your collection, and one you may find worth taking to a museum for an expert to identify.

4 All About Fossils

One day during a pebble hunt you are sure to pick up a stone with interesting marks on the surface, as if something had been pressed into it and left a pattern. The edges of the pattern will be quite smooth, so you will know that the marks are not scratches.

The marks are indeed a pattern – of something that existed there perhaps hundreds of millions of years ago.

When the world was young and the earth's crust was restless the first living creatures were already thriving in the sea. Then plants began to grow in the swampy ground and a few animals learned how to live on the land as well as beneath the water.

It was a dangerous time for all forms of life because earthquakes, tremendous storms, and violent changes in the climate constantly overwhelmed them. Disaster could strike suddenly. Masses of mud, sand and debris buried fish, animals, insects, plants and trees. More and more material, including rocks, was rapidly piled over the soft, watery tomb. The weight exerted such pressure that the debris enclosing the buried objects hardened. It did not always destroy and obliterate even the most fragile shells, bones, and leaves.

Inside the natural rock coffin the once-living matter slowly decayed. Tiny grains of silica seeped into the gap thus left, turning it into a stone-hard replica of the shellfish, worm, insect, leaf, and even large animal.

When you find this kind of fossil, called a *fossil cast*, it will look much like the pebble or rock in which it lies. The colour may be a little different, and if you could make chemical tests on the material of the fossil it would be different from that of the surrounding stone, but all the original material will have disappeared.

Another kind of fossil is called a *fossil mould*, and this you will frequently find as a tiny mark on quite small pebbles. Over a very long time water seeping through the rock dissolved all the parts of the trapped object, both the hard and the soft material, so that only the shape of the outside remained, perhaps the fluted lines on the outer surface of a shell or the vein marks on a leaf.

Not so easy to discover or to recognise are *trace fossils*. These are not replicas of actual creatures or plants but of the marks they made just before they were buried. They include such marks as the holes made by marine worms, the track of a creeping reptile, the smooth curve of part of an egg, or the wavy lines made by water plants brushing against sand as they moved in ocean currents.

The most exciting fossil find of them all is a *body fossil*. Teeth, claws, bones, and tree trunks may have decayed so slowly that there was time for chemicals to change their substance before the original material disappeared. Some of these relics were so hard, and were buried so deeply, that the objects are changed very little from the appearance they had when they were living.

You can never be certain that you will not come across, quite by accident, a very important fossil. Years ago little Mary Anning, who lived at Lyme Regis in Dorset, was enjoying a walk among the tidal pools below the cliffs when she noticed a large irregular shape sticking out of some recently fallen rocks.

She had found the fossilized skeleton of a sea reptile rather like a giant porpoise and called an *Ichthyosaurus* (fish lizard). The creature lived about 200 million years ago at the time when dinosaurs roamed about southern England. Mary's find was the first complete skeleton of this sea monster ever found in Britain. If you ever visit Lyme Regis you can see Mary portrayed in a window in the town's church.

Fossils can be as large as the biggest animals that have ever existed. But it need hardly be said that the fossils you

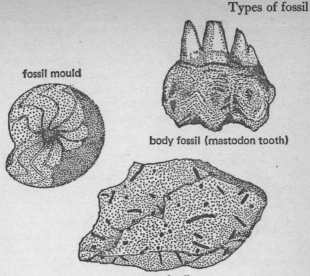

fossil mould

body fossil (mastodon tooth)

trace fossils

are most likely to find will be quite small. In chalky areas millions of them will be so tiny that they can be seen only under a microscope. Among them are larger shell fossils similar in appearance to those you can see on the beach with living creatures inside them, or only recently opened by sea birds, crabs and fishermen.

Recognising this kind of fossil is easy. But there are other patterns in the rock and on the surface of pebbles which you may not believe are the relics of creatures or plants which flourished long before human beings existed. There are tens of thousands of different kinds of fossils of the earth's earliest inhabitants. Nearly all were at least partly of quite hard substances and their shape could be preserved by sediment and minerals before every trace of them decayed and disappeared. Thanks to such fossils we can know something of what the world was like up to 3000 million years ago.

As water carrying sediment was the most usual cause of the process which ended with the production of a fossil, most of those which you will find will be near the sea, or in places where the sea once covered the earth. That means the fossils are of sea creatures and plants, and those living things which are mid-way between animal and plant, such as sponges.

With a little experience, some visits to a museum, and the studying of photographs many of them, as well as simple shells, will be quite easy to recognise.

Here are the most common fossils in Britain.

Sea creatures

Brachiopods. These shellfish have two shells, one larger than the other and in life hinged together so that the fish could open and shut its protective covering. An easier name for them is 'lamp shells', and they look rather like a tiny lamp with the rays of light spreading out in a fan.

Bivalves. These shellfish are familiar to everyone at the seaside, for they include mussels, cockles and oysters. It is easy to confuse a bivalve fossil with one of a brachiopod. But a bivalve has two shells which are the same shape and size as each other.

They are to be found in several different shapes and sizes. A strange-looking one comes from the beaches of Norfolk and Suffolk. This shellfish, extinct long ago, is like a half circle covered with fine lines and has a bump at one end. Local people call it the Devil's Toenail, a good name because it looks rather like a heavy claw.

Univalves have single shells and are to be found in many shapes and sizes. Those that are alive today include the snails on land or the whelks and limpets you can find stuck immovably to rocks in a pool when the tide goes out.

An interesting and quite common univalve fossil is shaped like an ice cream cone with a pattern running in a spiral from the pointed end to the hole at the other. You will find many of these fossils in the sandy shores on the East coast, but be sure that it is fossilized and not just the recently-abandoned home of a modern shellfish.

Smaller and prettier are univalve fossils like a decorated button coming to a point and patterned with delicate markings on the outside rings which decrease in size from the base to the point.

Ammonites. These are also single-shell creatures which must have been fearsome when alive, for their fossils can be too heavy to carry. The ammonite you will find is more likely to be easily held in the palm of your hand.

The name comes from that of a Roman god who wore the curving horns of a ram. An ammonite does sometimes look like part of a ram's horn, but more often the body is in the form of a coil making an almost complete circle like a sleeping snake without a head.

When ammonites swarmed in the sea they extended their bodies and could be twelve metres long. Asleep or when danger threatened they coiled up, and they are nearly always found like this. No wonder that people believed that they were snakes turned to stone before fossils were understood, and many stories are told to explain them.

Ammonites are quite common just below the surface in the land around Keynsham, between Bath and Bristol, and used to be turned up by ploughing or when rocky areas crumbled. To explain their presence it was said that more than a thousand years ago a Welsh princess was given land there. She planned to build a palace for herself. But the fields were infested with dangerous snakes. She prayed all one night that she should be rid of the reptiles. In the morning they had all been turned to stone.

You can hear much the same story if you visit Whitby. St Hilda was presented with the land on top of the cliffs to build an abbey (the ruins are still there) but she was worried that the numerous snakes she saw slithering through the grass might injure the nuns she intended to bring to the abbey.

Calmly she walked towards them. They all crawled ahead of her until they fell over the edge of the cliff, to be turned to stone when they reached the beach. Ever since people have been finding ammonites on the seashore below the abbey, and they are still to be discovered today. When visitors really believed they were snakes local Whitby people used to

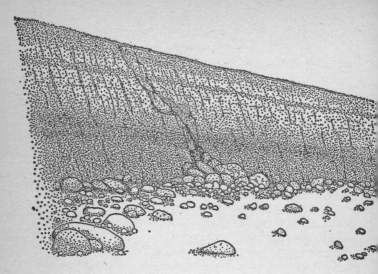

carve snake's heads at the end of the coil so as to sell the ammonite at a higher price.

Ammonites are much more numerous among the rocks near Lyme Regis. In the town you can see large ones used as wall decorations beside door posts and window frames, and small ones are sold in shops as paper–weights and ornaments.

If you come across a fairly large ammonite it will probably be just the trace of its shape on the surface of a boulder. Small ones may be intact. If minerals have seeped into them they will look as if they are made of a dull metal and make a really splendid trophy for your collection.

Belemnites are the small ancestors of the octopus and squid. The fossils look like bullets or cigars, pointed at one end and flat at the other. The pointed end was the hardest part and had a better chance of resisting decay, so you will often find just part of a belemnite fossil. They sometimes swam around in shoals. Quite often scores are found as fossils, lying higgledy-piggledy on top of one another and embedded in the rock.

Starfish are easy to recognise because the prehistoric kinds that became fossils roughly resemble those alive today. There are always five 'arms' on a starfish. You will, however, be lucky to find a fossil of a starfish intact. Their skeletons are very fragile and mostly the fossil is just of a piece of one arm, but quite easy to recognize because it tapers towards the end and is spotted with the rows of tube feet it used to move around and stick itself to a rock.

Crabs and lobsters. If you find a fossil of part of these creatures it is most likely to be a claw, which is very hard and resists decay. Complete bodies are rarely found exposed on the surface of a rock.

Bony fish. Fossils of fish are sometimes complete, or consist just of the skeleton. The bones will look much the same as that of today's common fish, even though the fossil will be of a kind of fish now extinct. Even if you are not very likely to find a complete fossil fish, you do have a good chance of finding a fossil fish tooth.

Teeth are harder than bones or shells and can remain unchanged except perhaps for minerals seeping in and changing their colour. Any recognisable tooth you find on a beach will probably be from a shark. In prehistoric times sharks swam in enormous numbers in the warm seas which surrounded and often flooded the British Isles. Their teeth were constantly replaced as they were worn down and fell out. Consequently a shark which managed to survive for years discarded dozens of teeth.

You can miss picking up a fossil tooth. It may have the appearance of a dirty-looking and rather shapeless object. A shark's tooth is usually covered with clay and dirt. The debris can easily be removed and then you will have a sharp, long tooth with the root still in position.

Good places to search for shark's teeth are along the Essex and Kent coasts, around the Isle of Sheppey, and in Herne Bay. There used to be so many on the seashore between Harwich and Frinton that local farmers paid children to collect them by the sackful. They were then ground down for fertilizer.

Trilobites. 500 million years ago, among the most

numerous creatures crawling about the sea floor, swimming to the surface to feed on floating weed, and creeping into rock crevices below low tide were these curious creatures, long extinct. Their fossils are in many sizes from less than one centimetre to five centimetres in length.

Trilobites were creatures with many legs or feelers, a hard head with large eyes, and an armoured body which some of them could roll into a ball, like woodlice, when danger threatened. But their most unusual feature was that the body had two grooves on the back from head to tail so that it appeared to be in three sections. This is why it has 'tri' in its name.

If you imagine a ladybird with its body divided lengthwise into three, you should be able to recognise the fossil of a trilobite. Some people suggest it is rather like a locust, and if you have seen a picture of this insect you will have another aid to identifying a trilobite fossil.

In the quarries around Dudley in the West Midlands trilobite fossils are still called 'Dudley locusts' by the workmen who often find them in the rubble of ironstone and limestone.

Trilobites survived for such a long period and in such vast numbers that their fossils can be found wherever the land was once covered by the sea, so you have an excellent chance of finding this easily recognised fossil almost anywhere in the British Isles.

Barnacles. You can see living barnacles fixed firmly to rocks washed by the tides, on the wooden supports of breakwaters and the iron supports of piers and jetties. Their remote ancestors which have become fossils look much the same – like small acorns. Often they appear as a small lump on a piece of flint.

Plants and Simple Forms of Animal Life

Coral. Coral is formed when the organisms create for themselves skeletons of limestone. Those which live in large colonies form the islands and reefs of the warm seas of the Pacific Ocean.

In times when the seas around and over the British Isles were warm enough for corals to flourish, huge numbers were buried and became fossils. They are not easy to identify because their shapes vary so much. It is best to search in those places which local people or the local museum tell you has coral fossils. It will invariably be where there is limestone, as they make their skeletons from this mineral. Salop is one good district, and Wenlock Edge in that county is in fact an ancient reef consisting of coral below the surface soil.

Sponges are another primitive animal with the appearance of a plant. They make their skeletons from tiny pieces of chalk or grains of sand.

You may be lucky enough to find a fossil sponge and quite easily recognise it because it looks much like the surface of a bathroom sponge with scores of small irregular holes. Another quite common kind makes a flowery pattern on the rock surface of a shell or rock. These are mainly traces of the holes the sponge burrowed in the rock or shell in order to obtain a firm anchorage and not the skeleton of the sponge itself.

Sea urchins. If you have gone on holiday in Spain or other countries bordering on the Mediterranean you will know what sea urchins look like as they are sold as food as well as lying dead on the sea's edge. Urchin is an old-fashioned word for 'hedgehog,' and these creature-plants have bristles or spines making them look rather like that animal.

In sea urchin fossils the spines have usually disappeared, and only the bare base will be found. One way to recognise a sea urchin fossil is that, whatever its shape and size, it will have fine lines radiating from the centre.

One kind quite easily found as a fossil looks like a tiny bread roll with the five lines marked on the top. It used to be called a 'fairy loaf', in the belief that it was food abandoned by the Little Folk who lived in rock crevices and caves.

Sea Lilies. In spite of their name and appearance sea lilies were creatures and not simple plants, even though they spent their lives attached to rocks beneath the sea.

The fossil looks like a closed tulip. Sometimes the tube, with its delicate threads which secured it to the rock, are visible. Sea lily fossils are found where there is limestone or shale.

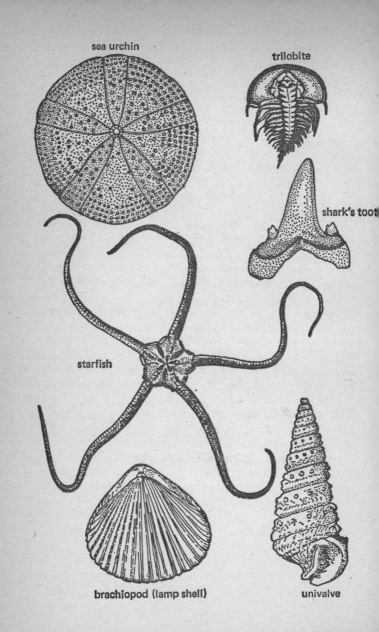

sea urchin

trilobite

shark's tooth

starfish

brachiopod (lamp shell)

univalve

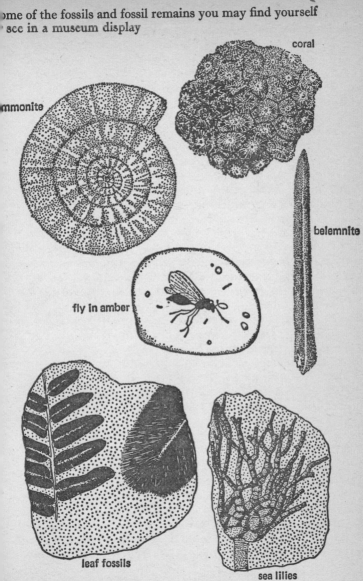

coral

mmonite

belemnite

fly in amber

leaf fossils

sea lilies

Graptolites were small animal-plants. Some moved quite freely in the water. Other kinds were attached to rocks. Their fossilised skeletons make marks on the surface of the stone. Tiny ones, dying while lying close together, leave such slight marks that they look like lines scribbled on the rock with a thick pen or pencil. Easier to recognise are the slightly larger graptolites which have the appearance of a very small, thin fretsaw blade with the teeth along one side.

Leaves. As leaves are so soft and fragile they were not turned into fossils except in conditions where the pressure of silt was very great as well as very sudden, with chemicals in the silt and rock to change the composition of the vegetable matter in a process called *carbonisation*.

Although the drowned and buried plants and foliage were so soft, fossils of leaves, fruit, twigs and even flower petals retain an outline of their shape, nearly always deep in the earth where coal and shale are found, for the same conditions which preserved them turned the prehistoric forests into coal.

Pressure flattened the object so that a fossil in coal or shale is usually black, shiny, and as thin as a flower or leaf that you press inside a book.

Coal miners find many of these fossils, which are always concealed until a seam of coal is broken up. You cannot go fossil hunting in a mine, but there may be heaps of abandoned material unsuitable as fuel which can yield a fossil or two. A better chance is in the shale which emerges from the surface of the land naturally. Pieces of shale break easily into layers when lightly tapped with a hammer. It is on the surface of a layer thus exposed that a fossil leaf may be found.

Unless you have permission to explore shale-bearing areas and places where coal mine debris is tipped, and you are always accompanied by an adult, you should not go hunting for these elusive plant fossils. They are so rare that you will probably be disappointed, and however careful you are the search can be dangerous.

Trees. Fossilized wood looks like wood in texture but not in colour, which is usually black. In fact it is no longer wood, all of which has long ago rotted away, and has been replaced by minerals.

Now that you understand how fossils are created you will realise that all coal is a kind of fossil, but so greatly transformed that the tree trunks and foliage from which it was formed cannot be recognised. Fossilised wood is rather different. It has not been so deeply buried or subjected to so much pressure, and most of the details of the living trunk or branch are visible.

Fossil wood comes from forests which once existed well above sea level. Then the land sank below the sea and the trees were covered by silt. Some of the land on which these buried forests grew then rose again. The remains can be seen in Barnstaple Bay and near Swansea when the tide is low. In rough weather pieces are broken away and can be picked up on the beach.

Much larger fossilised forests are still beneath the sea, but quite near the coast. In stormy weather numerous small pieces, and sometimes lumps quite difficult to lift, are washed ashore. There is one such forest off the coast at Lulworth Cove in Dorset (as well as remains of part of it on land at the edge of the high cliffs). Much larger, and therefore yielding more pieces of fossilised wood for miles along the coast, is the fossilised forest which lies beneath the sea off the coast of Norfolk near Bacton.

When you are lucky enough to find a fossil mould or a body fossil on the surface of a rock recently exposed by a cliff fall, or because you have broken off a piece yourself, it is probable that the fossil is quite fragile.

Attempts to remove it from the stone can easily break the fossil. Chipping it away is tricky and it is best to get help from someone who has the right kind of chisel and knows how to set about the job.

Even if the fossil is on a piece of stone small enough for you to carry there is a risk of the more delicate parts breaking away, particularly if you decide to wash away sand and dirt, and brush or wipe too vigorously.

An easy way to prevent this trouble is to coat the fossil very sparingly with a transparent waterproof glue. If a breakage occurs before you can do this one of the glues called epoxy resins will make a strong and permanent join, though you will have to be careful to get the joins exactly right if they are not to show.

Collecting fossils can always be rewarding whether you are in the country or at the seaside. You will be more certain of success if you find out beforehand if the area which you propose to explore consists of gravel, sandstone, chalk or limestone. A good atlas will tell you, and there is always a public library where the staff can show you reference books about the district's geology. If there is a local museum it will probably have displays of fossils with details of where they were found. Where one good specimen turned up there will usually be more for others to find.

There are the safety rules which we have already mentioned that you should always keep in mind when fossil hunting. Fossils, by their nature, have been hidden for an immense period of time. Most are revealed when portions of earth and rock are disturbed either by man, the weather or the sea.

If you are searching along a beach be sure that the incoming tide will not cut you off from the way back to safety. Crumbling cliffs should never be climbed, even for a metre or two just to reach a promising piece of chalk or sandstone, or you may start a serious fall. As we have already pointed out, gravel pits, disused quarries, and coal mine tips are always dangerous if you attempt to clamber up steep slopes of loose material or go too near excavated areas full of deep water, and all these places are privately owned. You will need permission to enter them.

Two or more pairs of eyes are better than one pair on a fossil seeking expedition. If you intend to break up pebbles or chip off pieces of rock it is wise to take a pair of goggles to protect your eyes. Those worn by factory workers are best, but as long as the lenses are made of shatter-proof glass or plastic, they will prevent sharp pieces of stone injuring your eyes.

5 The Hunt for Gemstones

Until you become interested in collecting pebbles you probably do not realise that on the beaches and among the stony regions near mountains, there are small stones which are beautiful and rare enough to be counted as gems.

All gems, such as diamonds, emeralds, rubies and so on, are just special kinds of pebbles. When they are difficult to find and have to be dug from deep in the earth, and lend themselves to skilled cutting and polishing to display their brilliance, they are called precious gems.

You will not find any precious gems, with the possible exception of an amethyst, but you have an excellent chance of one day finding a semi-precious gemstone, as beautiful and unique in its way as any of its scarcer cousins.

Then there are the stones which are so common that they can hardly be called even semi-precious. But they are so attractive compared with the majority of pebbles that they can also be called special. One trouble about discovering these stones is that when they are lying among thousands of other pebbles these semi-precious and special stones may be difficult to identify even after you have studied specimens in a collection in a museum or shop. Some of them can be dull and partly disguised with dirt and sand. They need polishing or even cutting to show what they are really like. What is certain is that there are far more of these pretty stones awaiting the pebble hunter than have ever been found, even if they have been searched for ever since human beings began decorating themselves with brooches, rings and other ornaments. There are miles and miles of seashore as well as huge areas of stony ground near mountains, the banks of streams and lakes, and rock-strewn hills where the keen-eyed collector has the chance of making a special find.

Now for the names and appearances of the stones you can find in Britain. We are going to include stones which do not strictly rank as gemstones. But all excel in beauty and, as they are not all that easy to find, will be of greater value for your collection than, say, a flint or chalk pebble.

Agates. These stones, with several kinds in the group, were gradually formed in crevices and cracks of igneous rocks. As they developed over a long period of time the layers are often in different colours. These banded agates, usually with layers of white and pink, are sometimes known as 'Scotch pebbles'.

Another kind is called moss agate, which looks as if wisps of moss have been embedded in the pebble which itself is almost transparent.

Amber. This is not a mineral, but originates from the resin of prehistoric trees. The resin oozed from the tree trunks, dripped to the ground and was then washed out to sea where it slowly solidified.

Pieces of amber found on British shores have drifted from the Baltic Sea. Very occasionally huge lumps worth hundreds of pounds have been found, but you will be fortunate to find a piece larger than a hazel nut.

Amber is either golden or pale yellow. It is soft and breaks easily.

Even a small piece may be specially valuable because of an object to be seen below the semi-transparent surface. Sometimes when the resin dripped to the ground it trapped an insect, preserving it for ever, just as it was at the moment of death. Usually the insect inside a piece of amber is of a kind which has been extinct for many hundreds of thousands of years.

Don't get too excited if you find a yellowish, almost transparent pebble and think it is amber, until you have made a simple test. Dry it thoroughly, tear up a piece of newspaper or tissue into tiny pieces, rub the amber on your sleeve and hold it a few centimetres above the scraps of paper.

If your pebble is amber the paper will fly up to it. If it is just a piece of coloured glass worn smooth by the action of the sea, nothing will happen.

The ancient Greeks discovered amber's powers of attracting pieces of dry material to itself. They did not understand that the reason was that friction on the surface of amber creates a charge of negative electricity. They called this yellow 'pebble' *Elektron*, and from that word we get our word electricity.

Amethyst. This is a form of quartz and probably the most valuable stone you are likely to find. It is transparent and coloured violet. After being cut and polished it shines brilliantly.

Aquamarine. A blue stone only rarely found today, except in Northern Ireland. It is blue-green in colour, like the sea on a day of hazy sunshine, hence its name, meaning 'sea water'.

Beryl. This stone is of the same material as an aquamarine stone and also of the far more valuable emerald (not found in Britain). Beryl is of a stronger blue than aquamarine, and the most common kind is opaque.

Breccia. In its natural state the breccia pebble is uneven and lumpy, but it can be cut and polished. It is dark green, almost black, with tiny patches of brown or red. The main substance in the pebble is quartzite, once broken into small grains or pieces by volcanic activity or heavy pressure and then cemented together with other minerals.

Cairngorm. The pebble is named after the mountains in Scotland where it is common, and is more exactly described as 'smoky quartz'. It can be pale yellow, orange or very dark brown, but whatever the colour it seems to have wisps of a darker shade which give it the appearance of having smoke trapped inside. The more transparent the stone – one in which you can see the 'smoke' most clearly – the more valuable it is. The weapons and decorations of a Highland clansman usually include pieces of cairngorm, cut and polished to appear as splendid jewels.

Carnelian. To check what this beautiful translucent (which means that it is not transparent but reflects light) stone looks like, go window-gazing around a few jewellery shops. You will be sure to see some signet rings with this stone set in them. It is usually a brown-red, but can be dark yellow or as red as blood.

On the beach a carnelian may not be easy to recognise because it is often coated with sand or mud and dulled by scratching. But on a sunny day, when held up to the light, the rich red glow of the stone will be seen even through the coating.

Chalcedony. Another pebble in the quartz family. It is named after a city in ancient Turkey, which you pronounce 'kal-sed-onny'.

The Greeks and Romans bought these stones to be made into necklaces and brooches, not only because they were beautiful but because they were supposed to bring good luck to the wearer.

Chalcedony from Turkey was green in colour. Any you find in Britain are likely to be milky white or pale yellow, but specimens are also found in other colours – grey-green, very light blue, or brown.

If it has not been subjected to much wear in the sea since it was formed in volcanic rock, chalcedony may have a lumpy surface. One way and another, chalcedony is not easy to identify, so you will need to ask someone who knows the stone to examine your find. A check after cleaning and holding against a bright light may prove beyond doubt that you have not only found a piece of chalcedony, but a rare one, because inside it is a trapped drop of water which moves about when the stone is shaken. The water has been there for millions of years.

Citrine. This is a form of yellow quartz, almost transparent and quite common. Some people call it 'false topaz', as it resembles that stone.

Fluorspar. Not really a gemstone, but its attractive colours make it a nice find. Though very common, recognising fluorspar is not easy because it can be found in many colours from an almost colourless transparency to very dark grey. The prettiest is violet in colour and known as Blue John. Many ornaments are made from this kind, and it is soft enough to be carved. Ancient Britons used to place ornaments of fluorspar in the graves of their chieftains.

Garnet. The usual colour of this stone is red, but it can be almost any shade from pale yellow to dark brown, with some tinged green. The only colour you will not find in a garnet is blue. Garnets split and break up quite easily, even though the material is hard, so you are unlikely to find a smooth, rounded pebble of it, but a piece which is lumpy and angular.

Jasper. This pebble is easy to find because thousands lie on our seashore amid the shingle. It is a kind of chalcedony, but coloured with impurities, usually giving it a red or brown pattern. The best find is of a pebble which is dark green marked with red spots as if it had been spattered with blood. It is known as 'bloodstone jasper'. If you hold this stone to the light the green will seem to fade and the whole stone becomes red.

Jet. Like amber, jet is not really a stone, but of vegetable origin, pressed until it became a kind of coal harder than anthracite. Ever since human beings came to Britain jet has been used to make ornaments, pendants, brooches and rings. If you find a piece of this rich black substance it will seem very light compared with a pebble of the same size, though it will sink in water.

Just to make sure that you have not picked up a sliver of a black stone, carefully break or cut off a tiny piece, grip it at the end of a pair of pliers and hold the flame of a match below it. If it is jet the piece will burn, giving off grey smoke which smells like tar.

Lava. This stone has the appearance of granite, but has a smooth surface. It can be dark brown or black, with white and pink spots. You will find it where there was once a volcano, and in its solid form it is known as basalt.

Luxillanite. One of the most beautiful stones you can find. It is granite mixed with feldspar and the main colour is a rosy pink with blobs of black. It will be found only where granite has been quarried.

Onyx. This is a form of chalcedony, but striped with bands of white and black, the stripes being perfectly straight.

Onyx is often used for cameo brooches, with a decoration carved into the surface.

Porphyry. Named after a rocky area in Egypt where the stone was cut to decorate the palaces and tombs of the Pharoahs, porphyry can sometimes be found in Britain where granite exists. Large crystals of a contrasting colour to the grey background are embedded in the stone.

Quartzite. This very hard stone is derived from sandstone, the grains cemented together and stained by the presence of iron. Quartzite is opqaue, and not easy to identify because the colours vary so much – white, yellow, brown, blue and purple. One way to confirm that your pebble is quartzite is to find another one, break it, and strike the broken edges against another. There will be a bright spark just as with flints.

You may hardly be able to believe it, but you can, with the right kind of brisk rubbing, produce this spark while you hold the pieces of quartzite below the surface of a bowl of water. Try this experiment in the dark, as naturally the spark is small and lasts only a fraction of a second.

Rock crystal. This transparent and colourless quartz pebble is common enough, but you can quite easily be misled and what you believe to be rock crystal could in fact be a piece of glass rounded and smoothed by friction in the sea. This is how you check: pick up a flint pebble – there are bound to be many of them wherever you find a rock crystal – and break it with another stone to get a sharp point. Draw it firmly across your find. If it is a piece of glass you will find it dragging on the surface and making a faint scratch. On rock crystal you will make no mark and the point of the flint will slide easily over the surface.

Sard and sardonyx. Sard is an opaque, rich brown kind of chalcedony. It is a very hard quartz and although you may see some jewellery made from it in shops, it is not often cut because of the damage it can do to the toughest saw. If you find a pebble which is free from any material adhering to its surface you will be impressed with its bright sheen. An interesting thing about a sard pebble is that when moved to and fro under a bright light its colour changes from almost red to brown and back again. Sardonyx is a rarer stone – a mixture of sard and onyx, the two minerals appearing as white and red-brown bands.

Serpentine. Though you are most unlikely to find a sardonyx stone in Britain (It is more likely to be onyx or sard) there will be no difficulty in picking up as much serpentine as you wish. Although there is enough of it to be used as a building stone, nicely coloured pieces are used for small ornaments and jewellery. It is of many colours – pale green, dark green, red, or brown with streaks and little patches of red, green and blue, as well as some marked with veins of white.

For your collection you will want to find a small and well shaped piece with plenty of contrasting colours. Serpentine is a soft rock and you must be careful if you try to shape it with a hammer as it may flake. It is better to search along the seashore near cliffs of serpentine and find a pebble which has been slowly worn to a smooth oval shape by the sea.

So much for the pebbles. Next some of the areas where they are most likely to be found.

As we have learned, pebbles drift for hundreds of miles, and this movement naturally applies just as much to gemstones, so there is always a chance that you will find them where there is no record of one ever having been picked up before.

But you will have better chances in those places well known as happy hunting grounds for the gem seeker. Here is a list of areas to check if any are near where you live or you expect to visit them on holiday.

England

Cornwall
Amethyst and quartzite on the beaches around Penzance and Marazion. Citrine on the beaches near Marazion. Amethyst, Carnelian, Citrine, Fluorspar on beaches bebetween Penzance and Marazion. Agate on beaches in St Ives Bay and Kynance Cove. Serpentine at Lizard Point.
Derbyshire
Fluorspar in the Peak District around the caves.

Devon
Carnelian and Agates on the beaches near Sidmouth.
Jasper near Babbacombe.
Dorset
Agates on the beach between Bridport and Weymouth.
East Sussex
Carnelian on the Crumbles beach between Eastbourne and
Pevensey. Agates on Brighton beach.
Essex
Amber on shingle beaches.
Humberside
Agates in bays near Hornsea.
Isle of Wight
Carnelian, Chalcedony, Jasper, Rock Crystal and several
other unusual stones on beaches between Whitecliff Bay
and Shanklin.
Kent
Agates and Sard between Ramsgate and Deal. Quartz at
Dungeness.
Lancashire
Agates on the beaches of Walney Island, near Barrow-in-
Furness.
Norfolk
Agates, Chalcedony, Amber and Jet on beaches from Sher-
ingham to Great Yarmouth.
North Yorkshire
Amethyst, Jet, Agates, Carnelian and Amber in bays be-
tween Whitby and Filey.
Northumberland
Amethyst in the Cheviot Hills near Scottish border.
Somerset
Agates are sometimes found on the coast between Clevedon
and Portishead Point.
Suffolk
Amber and Agates all along the coast.

Wales

Anglesey
Carnelian, Agates, Jasper, and Serpentine in bays around Rhosneigr.

Dyfed
Agates, Beryl, and Serpentine on beaches south of Aberystwyth and especially west of Cardigan.

Gwynedd
Carnelian and Agates on beaches along the south side of the Lleyn Peninsula between Abersoch and Criccieth.

Scotland

The mountains, streams, western islands, and the east coast are so rich in garnets, cairngorms and agates that there would have to be a very long list to name them all. If the area is stony and unspoiled by major roads or large towns it will be a good place to search. Apart from these almost limitless hunting grounds, below are some of the exceptionally good places:

Dumfries and Galloway
Cairngorm in the hills near Dalbeattie.

Grampian
Cairngorm in veins of granite south of Peterhead.

Highland
Amethyst at Golspie. Agates at the edge of the sea loch near Ullapool. Garnets on the coast near John o'Groats.

Strathclyde
Amethyst in the hills near Campbeltown, near Largs, and on the Isle of Arran.

Tayside
Amethyst, Jasper and Cairngorm between Montrose and Arbroath.

6 Giving Your Pebbles a Polish

Polishing some of your pebbles will give them a really splendid appearance. Of course, you will only want to polish the best specimens, and they must be of the kind of stone that can be smoothed and burnished. The likely specimens will be quite small, fairly smooth, and nicely rounded.

It takes quite a long time to get a really good sheen on a pebble when polishing by hand, so you will need patience. But it will provide you with a nice hobby for winter evenings and on those days when the weather is bad and you have to stay indoors.

First of all, be sure that the stones are definitely suitable for polishing. As you know, hardness varies, so some pebbles will take longer to polish than others. All quartzes are very hard but can in time be given a high gloss. Serpentine is fairly soft. Because of its contrasting colours it comes up beautifully after steady rubbing. Jet is quite soft and needs only gentle rubbing, when it soon takes on a rich, deep shine. Slate, though the pebble will be flat, is fairly easy to file to a nice shape and then rub smooth. Schists and shale can be be polished, but tend to split during treatment, so they may be disappointing. Sandstone is too crumbly to take a polish. So is chalk, unless you select a hard, rounded pebble and rub it quite lightly but for a long time.

Just so that you can see what a difference polishing can make to a pebble try the simplest method there is, and choose a pebble of serpentine, slate, or jet for your test. Get a metal-working half-round file (the kind that is curved on one side and flat on the other). A small one, about ten centimetres long, will only cost a few pence.

With the flat side, file away any lumps, dents, or deep scratches, catching the filings on a piece of paper, as you will be using them later. Use the rounded side of the file to improve the shape of the pebble and then thoroughly dust away all the granules of filed stone still present on the surface.

Now you need some wet-and-dry emery paper. Buy a packet which includes grades from coarse to fine. Dip the pebble in water, shake off the surplus and begin rubbing the pebble with a circular motion, first with a coarse grade paper and then with one or more of the finer grades. Keep inspecting the surface of the pebble to see how you are smoothing away the scratches. It should be quite smooth to the touch, though there will not yet be much of a sheen.

Next, make a paste of some kitchen scouring powder with a little water in a saucer. Spread the paste all over the pebble with your finger or a small paint brush. Wrap the pebble in a duster or piece of strong rag and rub the pebble round and round, unwrapping the cloth now and then and changing the position of the pebble. You will be able to see which part has not been rubbed because the scouring powder paste will still be sticking to it.

The pebble will by now have quite a shiny look, but you can still give it a real gloss. Tip the filings you have kept – there will probably be just a pinch of them – on to a saucer and add a drop or two of water, just enough to keep the filings together. Coat the pebble with this mixture and repeat the rubbing inside a duster as you did in the previous stage.

As you probably have only a little powder, you may have to scrape some off the duster and put it back on the pebble. If you don't seem to have enough powder, file some more from another pebble of the same kind and start rubbing again – quite gently but for as long as it takes to produce a good sheen.

Lastly, wash away all the debris sticking to the surface of the pebble in warm water containing a little washing up liquid. Rinse and leave the stone to dry. A final rubbing with

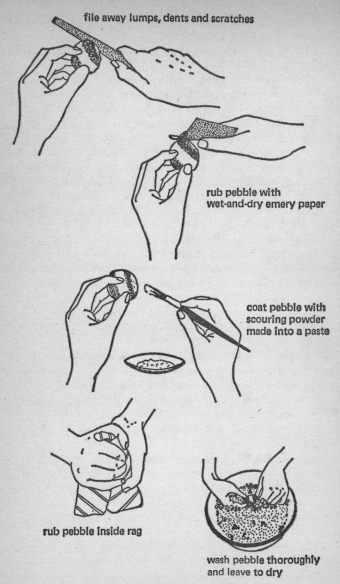

file away lumps, dents and scratches

rub pebble with wet-and-dry emery paper

coat pebble with scouring powder made into a paste

rub pebble inside rag

wash pebble thoroughly and leave to dry

The simplest method of polishing pebbles

a fluffy duster will give you your first polished pebble, and probably make you eager to try more complicated ways of polishing which will produce a really brilliant sheen even on harder stones.

These are the things you will need:

Three grades of carborundum powder (which is the commercial name for silicon carbide).

The best grades for your purpose are 220, 320, and 500. The numbers indicated the size of the granules, but don't worry if you cannot obtain grades with exactly these numbers. As long as you have three grades – coarse, medium, and fine – it will be all right. All good craft shops, many do-it-yourself stores and car spare parts firms sell these powders in little packets. The powder is just the same as that stuck on wet-and-dry emery paper.

A piece of plate glass if you are going to polish flat pebbles.

Don't use window glass or picture glass as it is too thin and will almost certainly break when you rub your flat pebble on it. You need only quite a small piece, say twenty centimetres square. A shop selling glass can usually sell you a cheap off-cut.

A pudding bowl of heat-resistant glass for polishing round and oval pebbles.

A small one, ten or twelve centimetres in diameter at the top, is all you need. There is probably one in the kitchen cupboard which you can have, but be certain that it can be spared, because your polishing work will tend to scratch the interior surface and spoil it for most kinds of cooking.

Two pieces of leather about ten centimetres long and eight centimetres wide.

The exact size is not important; the piece of leather needs to be only large enough for you to move your pebble about without going over the edge. Any bit of leather cut from an old gauntlet, handbag or wallet will serve if you have such things around. Or you can buy odd pieces of leather in craft shops. The main thing is that the 'wrong' side of the leather must not have a shiny finish on it, but still be in its natural state.

Tin oxide or cerium oxide.

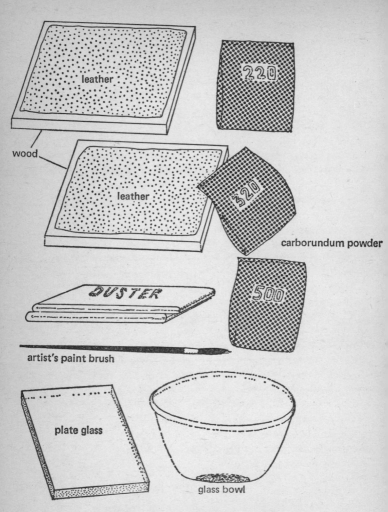

Materials for polishing pebbles

You may find this powder difficult to buy unless there is a good craft shop in your town. Even if your craft shop does not stock it, a helpful shopkeeper can order it for you. If you have real difficulty the firms whose addresses are given at the end of this book can supply you.

- Artist's paint brush and dusters.

First, we will show how you polish round or oval pebbles.

Fill the glass bowl with water, then tip the water away, leaving the bowl slightly damp. Put a level teaspoonful of coarse (220) carborundum powder at the base of the bowl.

Dampen your pebble by passing it under the tap or dipping it in water and then, holding it between finger and thumb, dab it on the little pile of powder and begin twisting and turning it, backwards and forwards, around the base and sides of the bowl. Continue for about a minute and then change your grip so that another part of the pebble is rubbed.

Go on changing position until every part of the pebble has been treated. As you do this the granules of powder will be spread all round the bowl, so that every so often you should scrape them back to the base of the bowl so that you can start the spreading once more.

This stage will remove the larger blemishes on the pebble and takes longer than the following stages. When you are satisfied that the surface is now fairly smooth, even if there is no sheen, wash your hands, the pebble and the bowl to get rid of all traces of powder. It is of no use saving it as the sharpness of the granules will have been blunted.

Make certain that you have really washed away all traces of powder before repeating the procedure with the next grade of powder – 320. This time you should not rub so vigorously or press quite so hard, and there is no need to work so long. This sequence will begin to reveal a really fine surface and when you wash away the powder from hands, bowl and pebble there will be the first definite signs of a polish.

Now you need your first piece of leather. As it is liable to curl during use, particularly if it is thin, it is a good idea to stick it to a piece of flat wood, shiny side downwards.

Dampen the 'wrong' side of the leather – the side that is

quite absorbent – with a little water. Don't use more water than soaks in immediately. Sprinkle on some fine grade (500) carborundum powder and start rubbing with a round-and-round movement once more. The granules of powder will get embedded in the leather, and you will be able to use this piece of leather again and again, adding a little more powder each time. Periodically wash and dry the pebble so you can check that even faint scratch marks are disappearing. In places where they still show, alter your grip and rub away at that part.

You will now use your second piece of leather, which, like the other one, should be stuck to a piece of wood. After the usual washing to get rid of all traces of powder, prepare a paste of tin oxide or cerium oxide in a saucer, using only enough water to make a thin cream. With a small paint brush dab the paste all over the pebble. So that you can get the paste all over the surface it is a good idea to hold the pebble with a pair of pliers, and move it around to cover any bare spots.

Rub vigorously on the leather. As you do so the friction will dry the paste and shiny patches will appear. Where parts remain dull change position so that they rub against the leather.

Continue rubbing vigorously for a time, gradually doing so more and more lightly. If dull patches still remain dab on a little more paste and repeat the process.

A final rub inside a dry, soft duster and you should have a polished pebble to be proud of, shining and glistening in a way you probably doubted you would ever achieve.

For flat stones the method is really just the same – two rubbings with two grades of powder on your piece of plate glass, one rubbing with the fine grade of powder on leather, and the final polishing with tin or cerium oxide on leather. The only difference is that as you are rubbing against the flat surface of the piece of plate glass you do not grip the pebble between thumb and forefinger but press down on it with two fingers.

Place the glass on a perfectly flat and firm table. If the piece is small and liable to move about it may be best to stick it to a heavy piece of wood. Dampen the centre of the glass and pour a teaspoonful of powder on the damp spot. Place the pebble on the powder and twist it this way and that, constantly reversing direction and moving outwards as the powder spreads over the glass. Wash and dry the pebble now and then to see how you are getting on, and when one side seems to be completed reverse and rub the other side (that is, if you intend to polish both sides, though this is not really necessary if you mean to lay it on a cotton wool base in a display).

As you are working on a flat surface the powder will be rapidly spread all over the glass, and it should be regularly scraped back to the centre with a knife or spoon.

Although polishing stones in this way does not take quite so long as you may think until you have actually tried it, you can, of course, only deal with one pebble at a time. Some of your most attractive pebbles may be too hard, too large, or irregularly shaped for you to succeed without long and tiring hours of rubbing. One day, perhaps, you will want to polish a whole collection of stones, including the very hard gemstones you may be lucky enough to find. This will mean using a tumble polisher, which has an electric motor turning a revolving barrel. It can turn out stones with a beautiful sheen and shape quite good enough to be set in jewellery and ornaments.

A tumble polisher is quite expensive, costing anything from £25 upwards, so it would have to be a special birthday or Christmas present. Or you could go shares on the cost with some of your pebble collecting friends – and it is certain that every pebble collector soon finds other enthusiasts when out exploring in places known to have worthwhile trophies.

Not many shops stock tumble polishers, except some in seaside towns where the coast is famous for its beautiful stones, and many collectors, young and old, amateur and professional, are regular visitors. But good craft shops will know where to order a machine, and there are some firms which can supply one by post. You will find some addresses at the back of this book.

Any supplier of the machine will also be able to sell the

How to polish pebbles

rub the pebble round the bowl

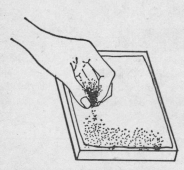

sprinkle fine grade carborundum powder on the damp leather

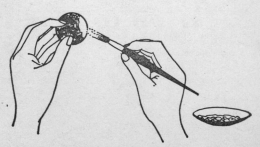

dab paste of cerium oxide on pebble

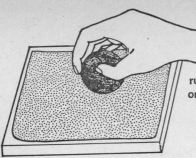

rub pebble covered in paste
on second piece of leather

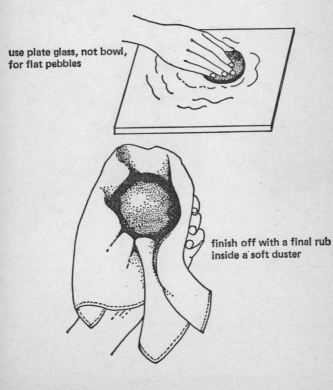

use plate glass, not bowl,
for flat pebbles

finish off with a final rub
inside a soft duster

grits which are used in the barrel to polish the stones. These grits are quite cheap and last a long time before they need replacing. What a tumble machine does is to imitate the action of the tides and the natural movements of pebbles in ideal conditions so that the polishing process is speeded up, and pebbles are smoothed in days in a way that would take years on the seashore.

But the speed is not so great as you might hope. Polishing by machine takes anything from two weeks to a month, depending on the roughness or shape of the pebbles and their hardness. The small electric motor of the machine is running for all this time, except when the grits used to polish the pebbles are changed and the pebbles washed. So the machine will use quite a lot of electricity and the slight rumble it makes will be heard day and night.

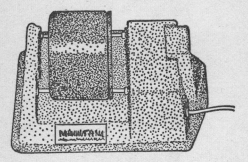

A tumble polisher

Still, it is interesting to know how a tumble machine works. The barrel, which is shaped like a cylinder and is usually about as large as a $1\frac{1}{2}$ or 2 litre fruit drink bottle, can be unsealed at one end. As many pebbles as will make it three-quarters full are put in, with enough water just to cover them. Then a teaspoon or two of carborundum grit is added, the cylinder is closed and the machine switched on. The barrel turns quite slowly, tumbling the stones against one another and the grit.

After about a week the cylinder is removed and opened. The pebbles will be getting smooth and there will be a lot of sludge. This has to be rinsed away through a sieve and the pebbles washed. This is a job to do out of the house, for the sludge will block the drain in a sink. Two more tumbling stages follow, using finer grades of carborundum powder just as in hand polishing, and finally there is a short period with the polishing process using cerium oxide.

You will see that using a tumble machine involves quite a long time and plenty of attention. Buying one is really only justified if you have many stones, including semi-precious gems, to polish. For quite a time ahead, as you are at the start of your pebble collecting hobby, you will probably be perfectly happy polishing your stones one by one.

There is no need to forget entirely the possible thrill of seeing your finest specimens emerge from their weeks of machine tumbling, highly polished and without a blemish. You may be lucky enough to attend a school where a tumble machine is part of the equipment in the crafts classroom, and in larger cities there are evening courses during the winter in lapidary (cutting, polishing and engraving) and jewellery crafts, where these machines are used for instruction, and students can bring their own specimens for polishing.

When we talk about polishing stones there is also the question of cutting them. Those, such as cairngorms and agates, which you may see set in jewellery in shops specialising in selling stones found in Britain, have usually been cut to obtain the right size and shape.

This is a job for the expert who uses special electrically driven circular saws with expensive diamond-dust paste embedded in the teeth of the saw. You may be tempted to try cutting a pebble with an ordinary fretsaw or one of those advertised as cutting anything from wood to hard metal. The only advice to give is – don't! Only soft stones will take a cut, and the pebble will probably crack or crumble as the cut deepens. On harder stones you will just ruin the saw blade, and you will be very clever if you do not cut your fingers before you give up your attempt when you find it impossible to hold a small pebble so that the cut will be in the place you want it to be.

Really, there is no need to think about cutting. Choose pebbles which have already been shaped to the size you want by natural forces and be content with polishing by hand. You can, with patience, get results as good as those achieved by all these expensive cutting and polishing machines when all you you wish is to have some beautiful, glittering pebbles on display just as they are, as Nature intended, and not in fancy shapes of metal settings.

The exception will come on that memorable day when you find a really valuable stone – a garnet, topaz, or even an amethyst. It may then be necessary to have it cut to bring out the beauty of the stone and make it to the best shape and size. That means finding a lapidary, a professional cutter of precious stones. In London and other big cities – notably Birmingham which has long been a centre of the jewellery trade – this will be quite easy. Elsewhere you will have to find a jeweller who specialises in repairing and re-setting stones. He probably does not do the work himself, but sends it away to a specialist.

The cutting will not be cheap, but if the jeweller, from his experience, confirms that you have a good stone which will be transformed into an attractive jewel, it is well worth setting in metal as a brooch or ring. Then you will have a unique gift for someone. While you wait for that red-letter day when you find such a stone, prove to yourself that cutting and shaping by your own skill is possible in just one instance.

That is with slate. Wait until you find a nice flat pebble of slate. If it has faint bands of colour in shades of green and black in it, so much the better. Decide on a simple design to serve as a pendant – a circle, oval, rectangular shape with the corners curved, a cross, triangle or even a star. Hand polish as already described to make sure the surface can be made smooth and glossy.

How to make a slate pendant

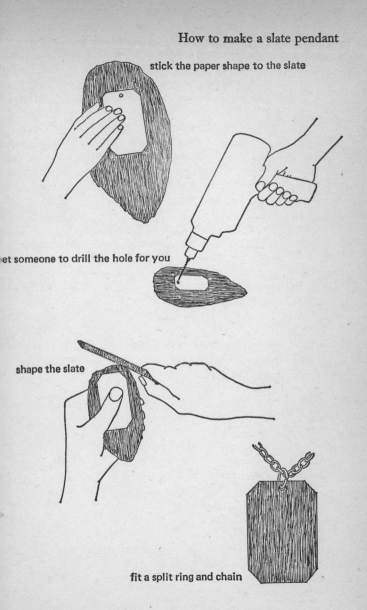

stick the paper shape to the slate

et someone to drill the hole for you

shape the slate

fit a split ring and chain

Cut out your shape in paper and stick on the pebble. Tackle the most tricky and accident-prone job first in case the stone splits. This is to pierce a tiny hole for the metal ring, cord, or chain on which to hang the pendant. It needs a fine drill held very steady and turning at high speed. If your father or some friend has an ordinary electric drill your problems will be over.

With the problem of piercing the hole overcome, you can start shaping the slate to the pattern, filing away with the half-round file, and perhaps other shapers in the tool chest which will make the work easier. Provided the file is a fine one there should not be any risk of cracking or splitting the pebble.

The shape completed, all that remains is to polish the filed edges and you have your own cut and polished stone. A finishing touch can be to buy a small split ring in silver or imitation gold from a jeweller to insert through the hole. He can also supply a chain or cord with a proper clip as the necklace to which the ring and slate pendant is attached.

7 Pebbles on Display

A simple way to show your pebbles is to clear the lower shelf of a bookcase, cover it with thick white paper held in place by drawing pins, and arrange your specimens with a little label in front of each, with the details on a card five centimetres long by five centimetres wide and folded across the centre so that it stands upright.

If you do not want to remove the books from your bookcase you could think about fixing shelves to the wall. Do-it-yourself shops sell slotted metal uprights into which brackets are inserted to space shelves as you wish. The only difficult part is fixing the two uprights at the same level and making sure that they are both vertical. The wall has to be drilled to take a plug for the screws, so for this you will probably need help – not forgetting to get approval in making your shelves a permanent fixture on the wall!

Shelves to go on the brackets can be bought ready cut and finished. They are a little more expensive than prepared softwood, which you have to buy to the right length and then paint or varnish. The useful point about these adjustable shelves is that you can change their position, and you can have as many as you wish, with wide or narrow gaps between them.

If you have some spare cash or are due for a birthday or Christmas present it is worthwhile looking round second-hand furniture shops and market stalls for little cabinets or chests of drawers which our great grandparents used to have for keeping bits and pieces in. These cabinets usually have two to four shallow drawers and are small enough to be kept on a table or shelf.

There is a modern version of the same sort of cabinet, sold for use in offices in which to keep letter paper, carbon paper, and so on. The best ones are made of metal and the really modern ones are brightly coloured. As the drawers are at least five centimetres deep they are ideal for storing pebbles in a dust-free condition where they can also be examined easily without disturbing their arrangement.

If you can use a tenon saw it is quite easy to construct rows of little square recesses to fit inside a drawer or shallow box which is to contain your display of pebbles. Measure the length, breadth, and depth on the inner sides of the container. Decide how large you want the square to be to take your pebbles. It will be best to measure the length and breadth of the largest in your collection and take that as the minimum size for a square, plus a little extra so that it fits in easily. If your biggest pebble is four centimetres across its largest dimension, for example, then your squares should be at least five centimetres long and wide. But this size for the squares will not always be exactly right because they must fit into your container, both across and up and down.

Take the dimensions of the interior of your container: let us say that it is 33 centimetres wide and 50 centimetres long. This is fine for the length, because 5 goes into 50, giving you 10 squares. The nearest division for the width is 6 squares, leaving 3 centimetres over. The simplest thing to do is to make the last row of squares into oblongs of 5 centimetres by 8 centimetres. But if you are clever at measuring you can make the squares at each end 5 centimetres by $6\frac{1}{2}$ centimetres.

Now you are ready for the actual woodcutting. You can use thin plywood or hardboard. First cut out strips just a little narrower than the depth of your container. If, in the typical drawer mentioned, the depth is 8 centimetres, cut your strips 7 centimetres wide.

Next cut the strips to go from front to back of the container. In the case of the drawer we are taking as an example this means the strips will be 50 centimetres long. With a pencil or ballpoint pen mark the strip at 5 centimetre intervals, the lines going exactly half way across the width of the strip, which in our example is 3·5 centimetres.

Cut the strips to go across in the same way, marking the half-way cuts. If you have decided to have larger oblongs at one end then start your marking to allow for this – in our example 8 centimetres along for large oblongs on one side or 6½ centimetres along if you intend to have oblongs at each end.

Remembering that the sides of the container will partly form the outside squares, you can work out how many strips of both kinds you need to make and how many cuts you will have to make on each of them. In our example there will be 9 cuts on the long strips and 5 cuts on the short ones.

Clean up the cuts with a piece of glass paper so that they are smooth and neat.

Fit the strips together by holding a short strip with its cuts upward and then pressing the long strip, cuts downwards, into the short strip. Go on fitting the remaining long strips. Then turn them all over and continue fitting the remaining short strips.

So long as your cuts have been straight, go down exactly half way in every case, and you have cleaned up any rough edges with glass paper, the complete work will be quite rigid and need no glue. And if you have cut the strips to the right length they will fit into your container and will not be loose. However, it is difficult to make a perfect fit and it will help if you just smear the ends of all the strips with a little glue

It will improve the appearance of your display if you then paint the interior of the container and all the squares white. Apply the paint sparingly so that you do not get blobs and wavy runs, and after the first coat is dry apply another.

Your pebbles will look better, each in its own recess, if you lay it on a piece of cotton wool. Write the pebble's name, and its reference letter or number if you are also keeping a map and book record, on a piece of thin card. If you aren't doing this, then just add the place of discovery and the date, like this:

SERPENTINE
Mullion, Cornwall
August 12, 1980

How to make divided sections from plywood or hardboard inside a two drawer display cabinet for your pebbles and fossils.

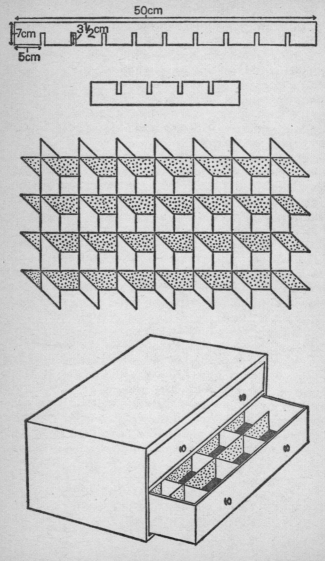

Cut the card to the width of the square so that it just slips into the recess. Typing looks best, and if there is no typewriter at home try to persuade a friend or relative to type the cards for you.

Another attractive idea for making up a display of small pebbles is to mount them as a picture to hang vertically on a wall. There is probably an old picture or framed photograph with broken glass tucked away somewhere in the house, or you can pick one up very cheaply in shops selling second-hand goods.

You don't need the glass. If the frame is shabby and chipped rub away any paint and smooth down dents with glass paper. Remove any brads or nails which held the glass in position. Paint the frame in a strong colour – black, dark blue or dark red.

The backing of an old picture or photograph may be of good plywood, but is more likely to be cardboard. If it is plywood you may be able to smooth it down with glass paper. Otherwise cut plywood or hardboard to fit on the frame. You can ensure the measurements are accurate by tracing round the outer edge of the frame.

After cutting out the shape and smoothing the edges with glass paper so that they are neat and a good match with the frame, paint one side and the edges white. When the paint is thoroughly dry fix the board to the frame with panel pins or a strong glue, not forgetting that you are going to mount the pebbles on the painted side.

The most attractive pebble picture is quite small – say fifteen centimetres by twenty centimetres – taking twelve pebbles in four rows of three in each row.

To stick them securely in a position on the board, which will be vertical when you hang the picture on the wall, it is best to use an epoxy resin adhesive such as Araldite. This is rather more difficult to use than ordinary glues, as it is supplied in two separate tubes, one containing a resin and the other a hardener. You have to mix a little of both of them on a tin lid or a piece of wood with a matchstick, and then spread a little of the mixture on each surface to be glued together.

You need very little adhesive. Just spread it on the part of the pebble you intend to go face downwards and on the spot where it is to be placed on your board. The mixed adhesive remains usable for more than an hour, so there is no need to rush the job and spoil it, but remember that once your pebble and the sticky place on the board touch they will immediately start to bond, and there is little chance of adjusting the position of the pebble when that happens.

As the pebble picture is intended to be decorative it may look better without any labelling. You can keep a key diagram handy for visitors and your own information. If you prefer to show the identity of the pebbles, keep the labels as small as possible, writing them in small neat letters on thin coloured card – say light blue or light green which will stand out on the white background.

Apart from collecting pebbles in order to obtain as wide an assortment as you can find, you can make some attractive ornaments with them, particularly with those which you have been able to polish. If you would like to use pebbles as ornaments bear this in mind during your hunting. Look for

A pebble picture

nicely shaped pebbles, usually smaller than your geological specimens, and try to collect several of the same colour and as nearly the same size and shape as each other as possible.

Some kinds, such as gabbro, serpentine, and quartzite are prettiest when their interior is exposed, so you should also pick up some larger pebbles of these kind which you can break into smaller pieces at your leisure. When breaking pebbles for this purpose it is best to place them inside a folded piece of coarse cloth so that all the pieces are retained and there is no risk of a sharp splinter injuring your hands or, more seriously, your eyes and face.

You will have noticed how even pebbles which are quite grimy seem to appear bright in the water of a rock pool or stream. After you have cleaned and perhaps polished them they appear even more attractive when immersed in water. If you have an aquarium your own pebbles will look much better than the stones and plastic chips supplied by a shop to spread across the base. There are two points to remember. Firstly, be sure to soak the pebbles in several changes of very warm water and then rinse well in cold water to get rid of any salt if your pebbles have been picked up on the beach. Secondly, if you break up the pebbles then wash them through a vegetable colander to get rid of the tinier sharp pieces which the fish might pick up and which could injure their mouths or intestines.

Underwater pebbles also look attractive at the base of glass bowls or vases filled with flowers. The will also help to stop the water getting cloudy so quickly, as the decaying matter from the flower stalks will be trapped among the crevices of the pebbles, which can be washed when the flowers are renewed. A more ambitious flower vase idea is to stick a layer of pebbles round the inside of the vase. You need to use a transparent, waterproof glue. The cellulose kinds are strong, and easier to use than epoxy resins. It is awkward to position the pebbles if the vase is too narrow to get your hand in, although it can be done with an artist's paint brush to dab the adhesive on to the glass and a pair of long handled pliers or tweezers to put the pebbles in position. With a bowl or a wide vase you can, of course, press on the pebbles by hand.

Dab the adhesive on the inside of the vase placed upright for one pebble at a time, starting on the base and pressing the pebble, also with a dab of adhesive, on to the spot, holding it there for a few seconds. Cellulose adhesives are quick-drying so you will not have to wait very long before you start on another space. Turn the vase on its side and stick a row of pebbles starting at the base and going up to near the top. When the row is dry and the pebbles are firm, turn the vase round a little and stick on another row. Continue going round until you have rows of pebbles completely covering the interior.

With a glass bowl the same method should be followed, but as the bowl swells out half way up you will need to have larger pebbles in the middle of each row and smaller ones at both ends. Leave the bowl or vase for a few hours before you put water into it. If any pebble seems loose you can easily prise it out and stick it on again. Cellulose adhesives withstand warm water so gentle washing of the vase will not loosen the pebbles.

Yet another way to use your prettiest pebbles is to stick them on the outside of a table lamp holder, a plain china jug or a vase, a preserve jar, and so on. Just a few small pebbles stuck on in a spiral usually look much better than a complete covering. The best adhesive for this kind of decoration is the one sold for fixing tiles.

Pebbles can be both decorative and useful when growing house plants. A layer of small, brightly coloured pebbles lightly pressed into the soil at the top of the pot will hide the brown earth, and help to retain moisture without interfering with watering. Those house plants in pots standing in a dish which provides drainage and prevents water leaking on to a shelf look much better if the pot stands on a layer of very small pebbles, and this will minimise trouble from water-logged soil.

If you are interested in miniature gardens, particularly those with several cacti growing in a tray, you can devise very attractive 'scenery' with pebbles of different sizes and perhaps one or two larger pieces of broken rock to give a

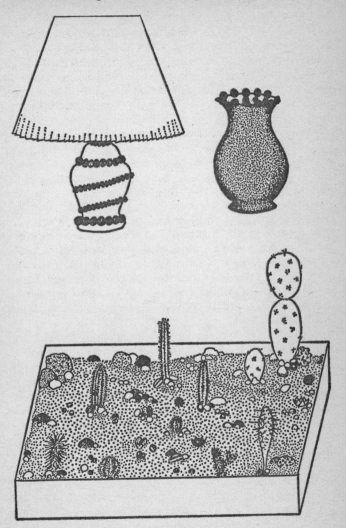

suggestion of the dry, rocky desert conditions in which cacti grow wild.

Of course you can grow flowering bulbs in a bowl of pebbles to provide some living colour in winter time and early spring. The best bulbs for this are crocuses and the narcissi called Paper White. You need fairly large and rounded pebbles which must be thoroughly washed to get rid of any salt and dirt. The bowl should be quite shallow, not much deeper than a soup or porridge plate. Arrange the stones so that they rest firmly against one another, with the larger ones at the top. Lodge the bulbs in the gaps among the pebbles so that their tops are just above the level of the highest pebble. With the small bulbs of crocuses this is easy. Narcissi bulbs are larger, of course, and you may have to arrange three or four bulbs on the bottom layer of pebbles and then press the top row of stones around them.

Pour in a little water gently, being careful that it does not rise high enough to touch the bulbs, or they will rot. The pebbles will become damp enough to moisten the bulbs. After about a week in a warm room their roots will begin to grow down to reach the water. Be sure to add a little water every two or three days (rain water is best; otherwise boiled water which has completely cooled). In about two months in the case of crocuses and three months with narcissi you will have a pebble-grown bowl of flowers.

Good fun for a long winter's evening is to make mosaic pictures with pebbles. For these you need very small pebbles, the sort you find mixed with sand and gravel. When you happen to be pebble hunting on a beach or in a gravel pit, fill a polythene bag with a few handfuls. When you get home you can strain away the sand through a sieve (remember, don't use the sink or you may block it), give the mass of tiny stones a good wash in warm soapy water, rinse in cold, leave to dry and then sort them into different colours and sizes.

Most of them will probably be brown, yellow or grey. If you want some contrasting colours in your mosaic you can obtain them by breaking up larger pebbles of sandstone, flint, agate and so on. Your mosaic picture will be most striking if you keep it quite small. The size of this book is ideal. Get a piece of plywood or hardboard cut to size, paint it white and after the paint is dry trace your design on it with a ball point pen or hard pencil.

Choose a simple design such as a five-pointed star, a circle, two circles overlapping, and so on. If you are more ambitious look through your books and magazines for a simple drawing which attracts you, and trace its outline on transparent paper, then transfer to your board by pressing sufficiently hard to mark the white paint.

The cement sold for sticking tiles on to walls is ideal as an adhesive. Brush it on carefully, not going beyond the outline. Then fill in the shape with the pebbles, selecting the smallest ones where the shape is narrow, as for instance, at the points of a star, and remembering to put contrasting coloured pebbles here and there. Be sure to get the pebbles as close to each other as you can. With tile cement you have time to move them before the cement sets, and you can adjust their position with a knitting needle or other pointed object. Very attractive pebble pictures can be made of a flower head, a

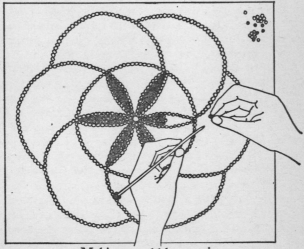

Making a pebble mosaic

butterfly with outspread wings, a parrot – any figure which is quite simple in outline but can be given a mosaic of many different blobs of colour.

In craft shops or in the homes of some experienced pebble collectors you may be interested to see examples of jewellery using pebbles, not necessarily semi-precious gems like carnelians and cairngorms, but ordinary stones of a good colour and shape, which have merely been cleaned and given a modest hand polishing.

Craft shops sell what are called jewellery settings or findings – tiny metal caps, jump rings, and cup-like bases of silver or imitation gold so that you can make bracelets, pendants, necklaces, brooches, and so on. For many designs there is no need to drill a hole in the pebble, though it will help if the stone is soft enough for you to make a groove in it. The only tools and equipment needed are a pair of cutting pliers, a pair of smaller ones called 'jeweller's pliers', and some epoxy resin adhesive.

Of course the stones have to be selected carefully. They must be small, nicely shaped, well coloured, and with a surface sheen. Once you get interested in using pebbles in jewellery you may discover that you are lucky enough to live in a city where there are evening classes in jewellery-making so that you can learn how to create more ambitious designs. These classes do not only give instruction. There will be the machines available to give your pebbles a high polish, to drill holes in them, and even to cut them to the standard shapes (facets) of the gem industry.

You will soon have many more ideas on how to make separate displays, once your pebble collection gets fairly big. If you intend to be a really scientific collector you could make separate displays of pebbles which came from igneous, metamorphic or sedimentary rocks. Or you could make each display a memento of a summer holiday or a successful day's exploration, helping in future times to remind you of that fortnight's pebble collecting on the Isle of Wight beaches or the wonderful day you had around Mount Snowdon.

You may want to make separate collections of special finds, such as fossils and semi-precious stones. At first these will probably have only a few specimens, so you need to allow space for additions as time goes by.

It is always tempting to go for quantity rather than quality. But every pebble you put on display should be of interest even to someone who is not a collector because you will have a story to tell about it. Merely to have dozens of pebbles, many of the same kind, can make you feel that you have been busy as a gatherer of stones but will not do much for your reputation as a clever collector.

Don't be afraid to remove a pebble from your display when you find a better one of the same kind. At first your pleasure in finding one of a kind you have not previously picked up will tempt you to retain it even though its shape is not good and its colouring and pattern are not as attractive as descriptions of the rock involved suggest it could be. There are nearly always better specimens than those you have, so you can constantly change your collection and improve it, making your collection more and more interesting.

8 Museums to Visit

Most museums with exhibits concerned with local history have a few display cabinets relating to local geology which will help you to learn about the sorts of pebbles you may find in the district. There are also many museums with especially interesting sections devoted to rocks, pebbles and fossils, with experts on the staff who will usually be available to help you on questions about your hobby.

Here are the best of these museums. There will almost always be one not too far away from your home and, better still, very often in your holiday area where you know good finds can be made. Most of them are free. Where there is a charge it is reduced for young people.

England

London. Geological Museum, Exhibition Road, South Kensington, SW7. As soon as you enter you can see a wonderful array of the rocks of Britain, because the entrance hall is decorated with ornamental stones from all parts of the country. Ahead is an arch of British marble.

In the centre of the main hall are displays of large and small stones of every known kind, including precious and semi-precious gems. On the first floor are collections of British minerals and fossils. Lectures with films and slides are held daily at 3 p.m.

Natural History Museum, Cromwell Road, South Kensington, SW7. In the east wing is a huge collection of fossils, including those of William Smith, who nearly two centuries ago was the first great fossil hunter in England. He described how layers of rocks had been formed at different times in bygone ages. There is also a gallery with a collection of minerals, rocks, stones and precious gems, and now and then there are illustrated lectures about them.

Avon
Bristol. City Museum, Queen's Road. Rocks, stones and fossils found in the West of England.

Cambridgeshire
Cambridge. Sedgwick Museum of Geology, Downing Street. Rocks, stones, ornamental marbles and fossils.

Cornwall
Camborne. School of Mines Museum, Trevenson, Redruth. Minerals, ores and rocks. Town Museum, the Cross. Local pebbles and fossils.

Truro. County Museum, River Street. A world-famous collection of Cornish stones and minerals.

Derbyshire
Buxton. Museum, Terrace Road. Local rocks, minerals and stones; ornaments made from local Blue John fluorspar.

Devon
Barnstaple. North Devon Athenaeum, The Square. Stones and fossils from the coast and moors.

Bideford. Municipal Museum, Municipal Buildings. Local geological specimens.

Salcombe. Sharpitor Museum. Exhibits are selected mainly to interest young people, and include a good collection of local finds.

Dorset
Bournemouth. Natural Science Society Museum, 39 Christchurch Road. Here is a wonderful collection of fossils from Barton Beds, famous for its marine fossils, and from the Bournemouth leaf beds.

Russell-Cotes Museum, East Cliff. An open air terrace devoted to geological specimens.

Lyme Regis. Philpot Museum, Bridge Street. Unique display of fossils from this area, famous for its finds, including large and small ammonites.

Essex
Chelmsford. Essex Museum, Oaklands Park, Moulsham Street. Collections of stones and rocks from the whole county.
Colchester. Town Museum, All Saints Church, High Street. Displays deal with the natural history of Essex and include rocks and stones.

Gloucestershire
Gloucester. City Museum, Brunswick Road. Displays explaining local geology.

Hampshire
Alton. Curtis Museum, High Street. Collections of local geological specimens.
Gosport. Town Museum, Walpole Road. Local geology.

Isle of Wight
Sandown. Museum, High Street. This museum is devoted entirely to rocks, pebbles and fossils from the cliffs and beaches of the island – a unique collection which is a 'must' for every pebble collector visiting the Isle of Wight.

Kent
Dover. Town Museum, Ladywell. Local finds from the chalk cliffs.
Folkestone. Town Museum, Grace Hill. Good displays of rocks and fossils.

Lancashire
Bacup. Natural History Society Museum, 24 Yorkshire Street. Collection illustrating local geology.
Manchester. University Museum, Oxford Road. Huge collection of geological specimens.

Oxfordshire
Abingdon. Town Museum, County Hall. Collection of local fossils.

Oxford. University Museum, Parks Road. Large collections of rocks and stones.

Salop
Clun. Town Trust Museum. Local geology in diagrams and specimens. This museum arranges tours for school parties.

Ludlow. Town Museum, Butter Cross. Fine collection of fossils.

Somerset
Axbridge. King John's Hunting Lodge Museum, the Square. Displays of stones, rocks and fossils from the Mendips.

Cheddar. Gough's Cave Museum. Exhibits include engraved stones and pieces of amber.

Taunton. County Museum, Taunton Castle. Collections or rocks and stones.

Wells. Town Museum, Cathedral Green. Rocks, minerals and fossils from the Mendips.

Suffolk
Lowestoft. Town Museum, the Prairie. Local geological finds.

Sussex (East)
Bexhill. Town Museum, Egerton Park. Collection of stones and fossils from the local coastline.

Hastings. Town Museum, Cambridge Road. Geology of the local cliff area and display of stones and fossils from the beaches.

Tyne and Wear
Newcastle-upon-Tyne. Hancock Museum, Barras Bridge. Animal and plant fossils.

West Midlands
Birmingham. Geological Museum, The University, Edgbaston. Rocks and stones, and one of the largest collections of fossils, especially graptolites, in Britain.

Dudley. Town Museum, St. James's Road. A gallery is devoted to geological exhibits, including fossils from local limestone and coal seams.

Wiltshire
Devizes. Town Museum, 41 Long Street. Collections of rocks and stones from all parts of Wiltshire.

Yorkshire (South)
Cawthorne. Jubilee Museum. Displays of local geology.

Yorkshire (West)
Batley. Bagshaw Museum, Wilton Park. Geological specimens from the Pennines.

Leeds. City Museum, Municipal Buildings. The exhibits of rocks and stones are world-wide in origin, but particularly concern Yorkshire.

Scotland

Borders
Peebles. Chambers Institution, High Street. Many specimens of stones and semi-precious gems.

Dumfries and Galloway
Dumfries. Sanquhar Museum. Local geology.

Grampian
Banff. Town Museum, High Street. A large collection of the rocks and stones from the Highlands.

Elgin. Town Museum, High Street. One of the best displays of fossils in any Scottish museum.

Forres. Falconer Museum. Specimens of rocks and fossils.

Highland

Cromarty. Cottage Museum. The museum is in the birthplace of Hugh Miller, a stonemason who taught himself about different rocks and stones and became one of Scotland's most expert geologists. The specimens he collected are kept here.

Inverness. Town Museum, Castle Wynd. Survey of the geology of the Highlands, with a big collection of specimen rocks and stones.

Lothian

Edinburgh. Royal Scottish Museum, Chambers Street. Scotland's principal collection of geological materials.

Strathclyde

Campbeltown. Town Museum. Stones, rocks and fossils from Kintyre.

Glasgow. The City Museum includes a gallery devoted entirely to geology.

Rothesay. Natural History Society Museum, Stuart Street. Rocks, stones and fossils from the west coastal area of Scotland.

Tayside

Dundee. City Museum, Albert Square. A large collection of specimens illustrating the geological formation of Tayside and the inland area.

Wales

Dyfed

Newport. Town Museum, John Frost Square. Local geology.

Tenby. Town Museum, Castle Hill. Good and varied specimens of rocks and pebbles from the beaches and mountains of South Wales.

Glamorgan (South)

Cardiff. The National Museum has a large collection of Welsh rocks, stones and fossils.

9 Some Useful Addresses

Maps and Handbooks
All good booksellers will be able to show you a selection of local and national maps produced by the Ordnance Survey and supplied through Her Majesty's Stationery Office (HMSO). They will have a list of all such maps and can order them for you if they are not in stock.

HMSO also publishes regional handbooks on geology. They are packed with information about the landscape, rocks, stones, and fossils, with many maps, photographs and drawings.

The region described in each handbook is:

England
  Northern England
  London and the Thames Valley
  Central England
  East Yorkshire and Lincolnshire
  The Wealden District
  South West England
  The Hampshire Basin and adjoining areas
  East Anglia and Adjoining Areas
  The Pennines and Adjacent Areas
  Bristol and Gloucester District

Wales
  South Wales
  North Wales

Scotland
    Grampian Highlands
    Northern Highlands
    South of Scotland
    Midland Valley of Scotland
    Tertiary Volcanic Districts

If you live in a town with an HMSO bookshop you will be able to examine any of these handbooks before deciding to buy it. Otherwise, any bookseller will order one for you. These shops are in:
    London. 49 High Holborn, WC1
    Belfast. Chichester Street.
    Birmingham. 258 Broad Street
    Bristol. Southcy House, Wine Street
    Cardiff. 41 The Hayes
    Edinburgh. 13a, Castle Street
    Manchester. Brazennose House, Brazennose Street

Equipment and Specimens
    When you wish to buy rare specimens of rocks, pebbles, gemstones, or fossils, abrasive powders for polishing, display cabinets, tumble polishers, and any other useful item, try to find a good craft shop in your nearest large town. Even if it does not stock just what you want it will usually have details of materials and products of suppliers and manufacturers and can order them for you.

Addresses of such shops are in the Yellow Pages of your local telephone directory under various headings: Arts and Crafts – Materials, Arts and Crafts Suppliers, and Hobby Shops.

Among the many firms which cater for pebble collectors, one may be near enough for you to make a personal visit (or you can send an enquiry by post, enclosing a stamped addressed return envelope). Here are some of them:

England
    London Arts and Crafts Unlimited, 49 Shelton Street, WC2.

The Rock Shop, Selfridges, Oxford Street, W1.

Brighton. Geobright, 28 Queen's Road.

Falmouth. Kernowcraft Rocks and Gems Ltd, 3 Webber Street.

Harrow. British and Overseas Minerals Ltd, 36 High Street.

Hull. Gemstones, 44 Walmsley Street.

Newbiggin-on-Sea. Rockhound Shop, 66 Front Street.

Southsea. Solent Lapidary, 145 Highland Road.

St Just (near Penzance). Minerals and Gemstones, Carn Glaze Farm.

Truro. Kernowcraft Rocks and Gems Ltd, 21 Pydar Street.

Watford. Allcraft, 11 Market Street.

Winchester. Wessex Gems and Crafts, Long Acre, Downs Road, South Wonston.

York. Derwent Crafts, the Shambles.

Wales

Cardiff. Ammonite Ltd, Llandown Estate, Cowbridge.

Scotland

Pitlochry. Lapidary Equipment and Supplies, Atholl Road.

Prestwick. Stones and Settings, 54 Main Street.

More Beaver Books

We hope you have enjoyed this Beaver Book. Here are some of the other titles:

Fortune-Telling Fun A Beaver original. A guide to all the different ways of telling fortunes, using numbers, paper, dice, dominoes or phrenology (the bumps on your head!) as well as the more usual crystal ball, astrology, palmistry, cards or tea leaves. Written by Gyles Brandreth and illustrated by Lim Mei-Lan

Beaver Crossword Book 5 A Beaver original. Eighty more puzzles by Pat Duncan to test your word powers and your patience, with the answer to the first Across clue in each case being the name of a bird

Flash Gordon versus King Vultan A Beaver original. Can you complete all the puzzles that will enable space hero Flash Gordon and his fearless friend Dr Hans Zarkov to rescue Dale Arden from the clutches of the evil King Vultan? Fast and furious action from the amazing Flying City!

These and many other Beavers are available at your local bookshop or newsagent, or can be ordered direct from: Hamlyn Paperback, Cash Sales, PO Box 11, Falmouth, Cornwall TR10 9EN. Send a cheque or postal order, made payable to The Hamlyn Publishing Group, for the price of the book plus postage at the following rates:
UK: 25p for the first book plus 10p a copy for each extra book ordered to a maximum of £1.05;
BFPO and EIRE: 25p for the first book plus 10p for the next 8 books and thereafter 4p a book;
OVERSEAS: 40p for the first book and 12p for each extra book.
New Beavers are published every month and if you would like the *Beaver Bulletin*, which gives a complete list of books and prices, including new titles, send a large stamped addressed envelope to:

Beaver Bulletin
Hamlyn Paperbacks
Banda House
Cambridge Grove
Hammersmith
London W6 0LA

321819